T0286701

From MDD Concepts to Experiments and Illustrations

LIST OF SPONSORS

From MDD Concepts to Experiments and Illustrations

Edited by
Jean-Philippe Babau
Joël Champeau
Sébastien Gérard

First published in Great Britain and the United States in 2006 by ISTE Ltd

ISTE Ltd
6 Fitzroy Square
London W1T 5DX
UK

ISTE USA
4308 Patrice Road
Newport Beach, CA 92663
USA

www.iste.co.uk

British Library Cataloguing-in-Publication Data
A CIP record for this book is available from the British Library
ISBN 10: 1-905209-59-2
ISBN 13: 978-1-905209-59-0

CONTENTS

INTRODUCTION

In the industry, system developers are faced with the following dilemma: reducing system development cost and time while developing increasingly complex systems. In the context of Distributed and Real-time Embedded Systems (DRES), development must retain a high level of quality when it comes to reliability, safety, real time properties, reusability, traceability, etc.

For that reason, Model Driven Development (MDD) methods and supporting technologies provide the techniques and tools needed to address these issues. The Model Driven Architecture (MDA) initiative of the Object Management Group is concerned with the development of standards and technologies that enable and support model-based system development. This book provides engineers and researchers with the opportunity to learn about Model Driven Development (MDD) and its application to distributed real-time embedded system development.

The book includes contributions from academic and professional experts on topics related to MDD practices, methods and emergent technologies. The development cycle of systems is based on the intensive use of models and model transformations on several levels of abstraction from system modeling to code generation. The contributions are a complementary of the presentations given during the summer school "MDD for DRES" in September 2006 near Brest, France.

At the core of MDE are models and model transformations. So, in the first part, we introduce general concepts about modeling (models, metamodels and languages) and how to implement model transformations. For DRES, the UML Profile for "MODELING AND ANALYSIS OF REAL-TIME AND EMBEDDED SYSTEMS" (MARTE) appears as a standard. So, two chapters give an overview of MARTE from the two modeling and performance analysis points of view.

Then the chapters of the second part of the book are oriented to "domain-specific" or "aspect-specific" concepts. We try to cover most of the common and important aspects of DRES development: structuring architectures using components, designing hardware architecture, evaluation and validation through tests and performance analysis. For the first point, we give an overview of several models of components for DRES. Hardware architecture and performance analysis arc respectively illustrated by a MDE approach for SoC design and models for schedulability analysis. Models for testing are then discussed from real-time and components perspectives. Domain specific MDE is then presented through automotive and avionic domains which integrate a lot of interesting constraints for DRES (distribution, safety, real-time).

In the last part, we give element of how and why using MDD. First we present a tool to support MDD. Then, the last chapter describes an industrial application of model-driven engineering concepts, deployed in complex developments, and their returns on experiments.

We hope that by covering all the development cycle for a wide range of embedded systems, we may offer information, points of view and experiences which will be useful when applying MDE approach on your distributed real-time embedded systems.

Jean-Philippe Babau, CITI-INSA Lyon, France
Joël Champeau, ENSIETA, France
Sébastien Gérard, CEA-List, France

CHAPTER 1

On Metamodels and Language Engineering

Chapter written by Pierre-Alain Muller

IRISA / INRIA Rennes
Campus Universitaire de Beaulieu
Avenue du Général Leclerc
35042 RENNES Cedex – France
pa.muller@irisa.fr

1.1. Introduction

Metamodeling is attracting more and more interest in the field of language-engineering [ATK 02], [KLI 05]. Meta-languages such as MOF [MOF 04] or Kermeta [MUL 05a], model-interchange facilities such as XMI [XMI 05] and tools such as Netbeans MDR [MDR 05], Eclipse EMF [EMF 05] or Software Factories [GRE 04] can be used for a wide range of purposes, including language engineering.

Defining a language with models can be decomposed in the following three activities: first expressing the concepts of the language (the abstract syntax), next specifying the meaning of these concepts (via mappings to a given semantic domain) and finally explaining how the language is rendered in a form suitable for the user (concrete syntax). Figure 1.1 outlines these main activities.

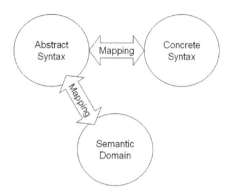

Figure 1.1. *Main activities of language engineering*

In this overview of model-driven engineering applied to language-engineering, we will use Kermeta, an object-oriented domain-specific language for meta-modeling. A running example, based on simple FSM (Finite-State Machine), will be used to illustrate the approach.

We will show how to express the abstract syntax of FSM using structural features, and how to express the semantic in an operational manner. We will also cover the mapping between abstract syntax and concrete syntax, realized with the help of a specific metamodel (and associated tool) for concrete syntax specification.

1.2. Modeling abstract syntax

Figure 1.2 presents a metamodel for these simple FSM (Finite-State Machines). An FSM is composed of states: it refers to an initial state and at least a final state and it can refer to a current state. A state has a name, it contains outgoing transitions and it refers to incoming transitions. A transition contains an input character and an output character and refers both to a source and to a target state.

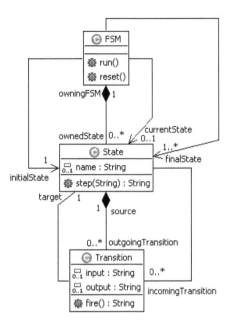

Figure 1.2. *Expressing the abstract syntax of FSM with a metamodel*

A given state-machine, such as the one presented in Figure 1.3, is then made of instances of the previously described metaclasses.

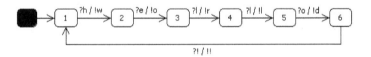

Figure 1.3. *A state-machine conforming to the FSM metamodel*

We may use a reflexive editor such as the one of EMF (see Figure 1.4 below) to create models directly as instances of the classes of the abstract syntax.

Figure 1.4. *Creating a state-machine directly as instance of the abstract syntax*

1.3. Modeling operational semantics

Abstract syntax defines the concepts of a language and their relations. However, abstract syntax does not give the meaning of these concepts. In our example we said that state-machines were made of states and transitions; however, we have not explained what happens when a transition is fired. Such a level of explanation is the purpose of the mapping between abstract syntax and semantic domain. The semantic domain can be seen as the virtual machine which will give meaning to the concepts of a language.

In our case, we will use Kermeta [MUL 05a], an object-oriented DSL (Domain Specific Language) for metamodeling, to express both semantic domain, and mapping between abstract syntax and semantic domain. Kermeta is an imperative language and therefore the semantic of the language under design is given in an operational manner.

The following excerpt (see Figure 1.5) presents the operational specification of the meaning of the step operation. The reader may also notice the use of constraints to express invariants, pre- and post-conditions. Altogether, constraints and methods constitute the description of the operational semantic.

```
class State {
    attribute name : String
    reference owningFSM : FSM[1..1]#ownedState
    attribute outgoingTransition : set Transition[0..*]#source
    reference incomingTransition : set Transition[0..*]#target

    // Declaration of the invariant : deterministicTransition
    inv deterministicTransition is
    do
        stdio.writeln("checkin deterministic")
        self.outgoingTransition.forAll(tr1 |
            self.outgoingTransition.forAll( tr2 |
                ( tr2.input==tr1.input ) == (tr1==tr2)
            )
        )
    end

    reference combination : Set<State>

    // Go to the next state
    operation step(c : String) : String raises FSMException is

    pre notVoidInput is
        c != void and c != ""

    do
        // Get the valid transitions
        var validTransitions : Collection<Transition>
        validTransitions := outgoingTransition.select { t | t.input.equals(c) }
        // Check if there is one and only one valid transition
        if validTransitions.empty then raise NoTransition.new end
        if validTransitions.size > 1 then raise NonDeterminism.new end

        // Fire the transition
        result := validTransitions.one.fire
    end

    post notVoidOutput is
        result != void and result != ""

    // Create a new state from self state
    method copy() : State is do
        result := State.new
        result.name := String.clone(name)
        result.combination := Set<State>.new
    end
}
```

Figure 1.5. *Excerpt of an operational specification of the semantics of finite-state machines*

This kind of specification is directly executable by the Kermeta virtual machine and the overall meaning (the semantics) of the language under design is expressed by the set of all such operations. As a consequence, any program (or model) written in terms of a language specified in Kermeta can thus be interpreted by the virtual machine. An example of execution is given below in Figure 1.6. Such execution capability is primarily intended for simulation purpose.

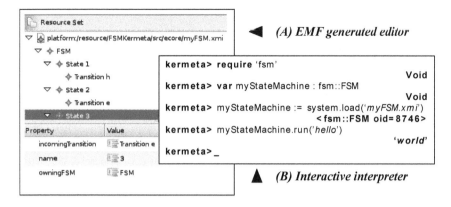

Figure 1.6. *Example of execution; "hello" is transformed into "world"*

1.4. Modeling concrete syntax

Concrete syntax is mainly intended for providing users with a convenient way of creating models. This can be done either in textual of graphical ways. In the following sections we will concentrate on textual representations, although the approach presented in this chapter can also be applied to graphical interfaces [FON 05].

Concrete syntax is traditionally expressed with rules, conforming to EBNF-like grammars, which can be processed by compiler-compilers to generate parsers. Unfortunately these generated parsers produce concrete syntax trees, leaving a gap with the abstract syntax defined by metamodels, and further ad-hoc hand-coding is required.

We present here a novel approach for the specification of concrete syntax, which takes advantage of metamodels to generate fully operational tools (such as parsers and pretty-printers). The principle is to map abstract syntax to concrete syntax via bidirectional mapping-models with support for both model-to-text and text-to-model transformations. This goes beyond uni-directional mappings such as [M2T 04].

Figure 1.7 summarizes the approach.

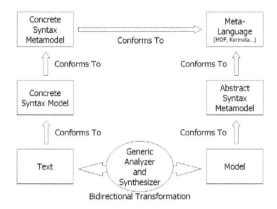

Figure 1.7. *A model-driven generic machine can perform the bidirectional transformation*

Going back to our FSM example, a typical textual concrete syntax for creating state machines conforming to the FSM metamodel might be:

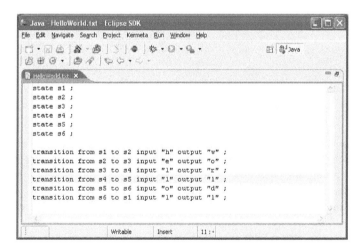

Figure 1.8. *Typical example of concrete syntax for state-machines*

In this example of concrete syntax there is no specific materialization of the FSM in the text (there is only one FSM). A state is declared by a keyword followed by a name. A transition is declared as a sequence, which starts with two keywords ("transition" and "from"), followed by the names of the source and target states (separated by the keyword "to"), and finally by the input and output strings (declared respectively by the input and output keywords).

Figure 1.9 shows how this textual representation can be specified under the shape of a model conforming to a specific metamodel for concrete syntax modeling. A detailed description of this metamodel is given in [MUL 06]. As we did for the abstract syntax, we may use the reflexive editor of EMF to create this model directly as a graph of the instances of the metaclasses (of the concrete syntax metamodel). A typical model might be:

Figure 1.9. *Typical model of concrete syntax*

As explained in [MUL 06], when reading text, the input stream can be tokenized and parsed by a generic parser which operates by model-driven recursive descent. Model-driven recursive descent designates a recursive top-down parsing process which is taking advantage of the knowledge captured in the models of abstract and concrete syntax. While the parser recognizes valid sequences of tokens, it instantiates the abstract syntax, and builds an abstract representation (actually a model) corresponding to the input text.

Conversely, when pretty-printing, text can be generated by a generic text synthesizer which operates like a model-driven template engine. The synthesizer visits the model (conform to the abstract syntax metamodel) and uses the rendering information present in the concrete syntax model (conform to the concrete syntax metamodel) to feed text to the output stream.

1.5. Related works

Model-driven language engineering is related to many other works, and can be considered as some kind of synthesis of these works, in the specific context of model-driven engineering applied to language definition. The paragraphs below include the major areas of related works.

Grammars, graphs and generic environment generators. Much of the concepts presented in this paper take their roots in the seminal work conducted in the late sixties on grammars and graphs and in the early eighties in the field of generic environment generators (such as Centaur [BOR 88]) that, when given the formal specification of a programming language (syntax and semantics), produce a language-specific environment. The generic environment generators sub-category has recently received significant industrial interest; this includes approaches such as Xactium [CLA 04] or Software Factories [GRE 04].

Model-driven environments. There are several ongoing efforts to promote the convergence of open-source model-driven environments, for instance: Modelware (http://www.modelware-ist.org/), TopCaseD (http://www.laas.fr/SPIP/spip-topcased/) and OpenEmbeDD (http://openembedd.inria.fr).

Generative programming and domain-specific languages. Generative programming aims at modeling and implementing system families in such a way that a given system can be automatically generated from a specification written in a domain-specific language. This includes multi-purpose model-aware languages such as Xion [MUL 05b] or MTL [VOJ 04], or model transformation languages such as QVT [QVT 05].

Meta-CASE systems. Meta-CASE systems, such as MetaEdit [SMO 91], Dome [ENG 00] or EMF [EMF 05], provide customized software engineering environments, separately from the main software components.

1.6. Conclusion

In this chapter we have presented how model-driven engineering may be applied to language engineering. Using the example of the definition of a language for simple finite-state machines, we have shown how abstract syntax, semantic domain and mappings could be specified with an object-oriented DSL for metamodeling. We have also shown how a specific metamodel for concrete syntax could be used to transform either texts to models, or models to texts.

Traditional language engineering is carried out in the grammarware technological space, i.e. it starts with the grammar of a language to produce a variety of tools for processing programs expressed in this language. We have presented here a radical revision of language engineering completely based on models, and thus severing all links with the grammar world.

1.7. References

[ATK 02] ATKINSON C., KUEHNE T., *The role of meta-modeling in MDA,* Workshop in Software Model Engineering (WISME@UML), Dresden, Germany, 2002.

[BOR 88] BORRAS P., CLÉMENT D., DESPEYROUX TH., INCERPI J., KAHN G., LANG B., PASCUAL V., *CENTAUR: The System. Software Development Environments* (SDE): 14-24, 1988.

[CLA 04] CLARK, T., EVANS, A., SAMMUT, P. AND WILLANS, J. *Applied Metamodelling: A Foundation for Language Driven Development,* http://albini.xactium.com, 2004.

[EMF 05] ECLIPSE, *Eclipse Modeling Framework (EMF),* http://www.eclipse.org/emf/, 2005.

[ENG 00] ENGSTROM E., KRUEGER J., Building and rapidly evolving domain-specific tools with DOME. *Proceedings of IEEE International Symposium on Computer-Aided Control System Design, CACSD,* 83-88, *2000.*

[FON 05] FONDEMENT F., BAAR T., *Making Metamodels Aware of Concrete Syntax,* in: European Conference on Model Driven Architecture (ECMDA), LNCS 3748, pp. 190–204, 2005.

[GRE 04] GEENFIELD, J., SHORT, K., COOK, S., KENT, S. AND CRUPI, J. *Software Factories: Assembling Applications with Patterns, Models, Frameworks, and Tools.* Wiley, 2004.

[KLI 05]] KLINT P., LÄMMEL R. AND VERHOEF C., *Towards an engineering discipline for grammarware,* ACM TOSEM, Vol. 14, N. 3, PP 331-380, May 2005.

[MDR 05] SUN MICROSYSTEMS, Metadata repository (MDR), http://mdr.netbeans.org/, 2005.

[MOF 04] OMG. MOF 2.0 *Core Final Adopted Specification,* Object Management Group, http://www.omg.org/cgi-bin/doc?ptc/03-10-04, 2004.

[MUL 05a] MULLER P.-A., FLEUREY F., JÉZÉQUEL J.-M., *Weaving executability into object-oriented meta-languages,* MoDELS, LNCS 3713, pp. 264–278, 2005.

[MUL 05b] MULLER P.-A., STUDER P., FONDEMENT F., BEZIVIN J., *Platform Independent Web Application Modeling and Development with Netsilon,* Software and System Modeling, Springer, Vol. 4, Number 4, pp. 424-442, November 2005.

[MUL 06] MULLER P.-A., FLEUREY F., FONDEMENT F., HASSENFORDER M., SCHNECKENBURGER R., GÉRARD S., JÉZÉQUEL J.-M., *Model-Driven Analysis and Synthesis of Concrete Syntax,* MoDELS, 2006.

[M2T 04] OMG, *MOF Model to Text Transformation Language* (Request For Proposal), OMG Document ad/2004-04-07, 2004.

[QVT 05] OMG. *Revised submission for MOF 2.0 Query/View/Transformation*, Object Management Group (QVT-Merge Group), http://www.omg.org/cgi-bin/apps/doc?ad/2005-03-02, 2005.

[SMO 91] SMOLANDER, K., LYYTINEN, K., TAHVANAINEN, V.-P. AND MARTTIIN, P. *MetaEdit: a flexible graphical environment for methodology modelling*. Proceedings of the third international conference on Advanced information systems engineering, 1991.

[VOJ 04] VOJTISEK D., JÉZÉQUEL J.-M., *MTL and Umlaut NG: Engine and Framework for Model Transformation*. ERCIM News, 58, 2004.

[XMI 05] OMG, *XML Metadata Interchange (XMI 2.1)*, OMG Document formal/05-09-01, 2005.

CHAPTER 2

Using Directives to Implement Model Transformations

Chapter written by Devon Simmonds, Robert France, and Sudipto Ghosh

Department of Computer Science
Colorado State University, Fort Collins, CO, 80523
{simmonds,france,ghosh}@cs.colostate.edu

2.1. Introduction

In MDE [Obj 03b, SCH 02, SIL 04, SEL 03, WAD 02] abstract models of systems are created and systematically transformed to concrete implementations. Two key principles of MDE are separation of concerns and rigor [SEL 03]. Most MDE approaches provide support for horizontal and vertical separation of concerns. Horizontal separation of software features is typically accomplished by modeling a system using views (e.g., the ISO RM-ODP framework 5)[ISO]. Aspect-oriented modeling techniques support horizontal separation of crosscutting software features (i.e., feature descriptions that are spread across and tangled with descriptions of other features) in views called *aspects* (e.g., see [BAN 04, SIM 05]).

Vertical separation of concerns is supported by providing mechanisms for representing system views at different levels of abstraction. The model driven architecture (MDA) initiative [Obj 03b] proposes a particular form of vertical separation of concerns in which platform independent models (PIM) are systematically transformed into platform specific models (PSM). The term platform typically refers to middleware technology, thus a PIM is a middleware independent model and a PSM is a middleware specific model.

MDE tools, languages, and techniques must be founded on formally defined concepts if they are to be used effectively. Adherence to the software engineering rigor principle is essential. This requires the use of formally defined modeling notations that are capable of producing analyzable models, and the use of verifiable model transformations.

Model transformations are key to the success of MDE techniques. A model transformation is a process that takes as input one or more source models and produces one or more target models. In MDE transformations can be used to (1) support representation of systems at different levels of abstraction (refinement and abstraction transformations), (2) restructure designs (design refactoring) and (3) obtain representations that are amenable to particular types of analyses (e.g., transforming a UML design model to a performance estimation model).

The Query/View/Transformation (QVT) standard [The 05] developed and maintained by the OMG provides a standard set of concepts and notation for describing model transformations. We used the QVT to define transformations in an aspect-oriented model driven development framework (AOMDF) [SIM 05] that we are developing. We found it cumbersome to use. In this chapter we propose an approach to implementing transformations that overcomes some of the QVT problems we encountered. We also give an overview of the QVT and its shortcomings.

2.2. Model Transformation Using Embedded Directives

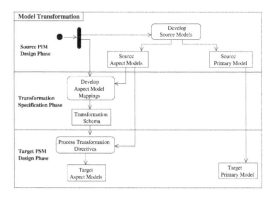

Figure 2.1. *AOMDF model transformation process using embedded directives*

This section presents a technique for transforming platform-independent class and interaction models to platform-specific models. The transformation technique is illustrated in Figure 2.1. In the figure, Source Aspect Models are a set of class and interaction diagram specifications of a platform-independent crosscutting software feature. Source Primary Model is the class and interaction diagram specifications of the core functionality of the target application.

The transformation of a platform-independent class aspect model to a platform-specific model is specified by embedding transformation directives in a class model. Similarly, the transformation of a platform-independent interaction aspect model to a platform-specific model is specified by embedding transformation directives in an interaction model. The class or interaction model with the embedded transformation directives is called a transformation schema.

The transformation is effected by executing the *Process transformation Directives* activity, taking the transformation schema and the source aspect models as input. The result of the transformation is the Target Aspect model for the selected platform. This Target Aspect model is application independent and can therefore be instantiated and composed with any application for which the bindings required by the aspect can be provided.

2.3. Transformation directives

The transformation directives embedded in a model specify relationships between model elements in a source aspect model and model elements in a target aspect model. The directives also specify how model elements in the target aspect model are obtained from model elements in the source aspect model. The transformation directives described in this section are: source, rename, exclude and new.

2.3.1. *The source and rename Directives*

The source directive is to copy properties from a model element in the source aspect model to a model element in the target aspect model. All properties of the source model element except the name of the element are copied. The directive has the form: **source**.|SAModelElement [renameDirective], where |SAModelElement is a reference to a model element in the source aspect model and renameDirective represents an optional rename directive.

For example, Figure 2.2 illustrates the use of the source directive. In Figure 2.2, model elements marked with the "|" symbol are model element templates.

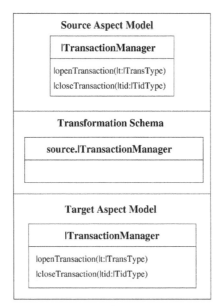

Figure 2.2. *The source directive*

The figure shows a source aspect model with a single class template (|TransactionManager), and a transformation schema with a class template defined using the source directive: source.|TransactionManager. This directive stipulates the creation of a new class template that inherits the properties, in this instance the two operation templates of the |TransactionManager class template. In the absence of a rename directive, the name of the target aspect model element defaults to the name of the source aspect model element. For example, in Figure 2.2, the name of the class template in the target aspect model is |TransactionManager. The source directive may be applied to classes, interfaces, operations, attributes, and their templates in class models and messages, lifelines, and their templates in sequence models.

The **rename** directive is used to give a platform-specific name to a model element. For example, to give the name '*Current*' to the class template in the target aspect model in Figure 2.2, the rename directive: source.|TransactionManager {name=Current} may be used. The form of the rename directive is: ModelElement {name = modelElementName} where modelElementName is the platform-specific name to be given to ModelElement. The rename directive may be applied to classes, interfaces, operations, attributes, parameters and their templates in class models and messages, parameters, lifelines and their templates in sequence models.

2.3.2. The redefine Directive

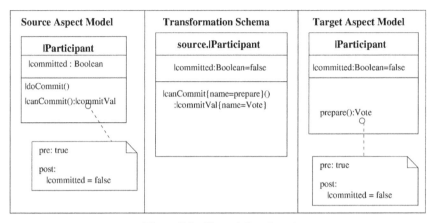

Figure 2.3. *The redefine directive*

When a composite model element (e.g., a class) is defined using the source directive, operation and attribute templates defined in the source aspect model element are copied to the corresponding target aspect model element. Operation and attribute templates that are copied may be modified by adding or omitting properties. New model elements may also be added to the class by explicitly defining them. For example, in Figure 2.3, the |committed:Boolean=false transformation schema attribute redefines the |committed:Boolean attribute template defined in |Participant by adding a default value. Similarly, the |canCommit{name=prepare}():|commitVal   {name=Vote} transformation schema operation redefines the |canCommit operation template defined in |Participant by specifying platform-specific names for the operation and the return type.

Whenever an operation or attribute template that is to be copied from a composite source aspect model element is explicitly specified in the transformation schema, the specification is a directive for the modification of the specified model element. This directive is called the redefine directive. The redefine directive has the format: ModelElement[renameDirective] where ModelElement may be an operation, an attribute or their templates.

2.3.3. *The new and exclude Directives*

The new directive is used to specify a new model element within a namespace. The format of the new directive is: new SAModelElement [renameDirective] where ModelElement is a specification of the new model element. When a composite model element (e.g., a class) is defined using the source directive, new model elements may be added to the class by explicitly defining them. The new directive is used to differentiate between a model element that is being redefined and new model elements. For example, in Figure 2.4, the directive: new join(id:Object) defines a new operation.

The new directive has an explicit as well as an implicit form. The explicit form of the directive uses the new keyword to resolve ambiguity by differentiating between new model elements and model elements being redefined. However, in cases where there is no ambiguity, new model elements may be specified without using an explicit use of the new keyword.

The exclude directive is used to eliminate a model element from a namespace in the target aspect model. For example, in Figure 2.4, the directive: exclude |openTransaction (|t:|TransType) specifies that this operation template should be omitted from the target aspect model. The exclude directive may be applied to operations, attributes, parameters and their templates in class models and messages, parameters and their templates in sequence models.

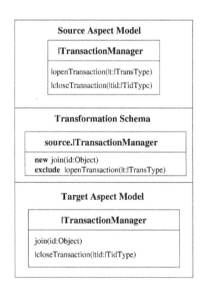

Figure 2.4. *The new and exclude directives*

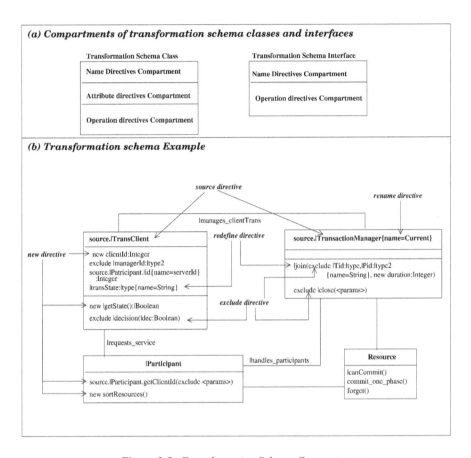

Figure 2.5. *Transformation Schema Compartments*

2.4. Transformation schemas

Transformation schemas are used to specify directives that are used in transforming a source aspect model to a target aspect model. Every statement in a transformation schema is a directive. The model elements being transformed may be composite or non-composite. Composite elements include classes and interfaces while operations and attributes are non-composite. A composite transformation schema model element is divided into compartments as shown in Figure 2.5 (a). A transformation schema class is divided into three compartments: *a name directive compartment, an attribute directive compartment* and *an operation directive compartment*. Transformation schema interfaces do not have attribute compartments. Each statement in a name directive compartment resolves to a model element name when processed.

Each statement in an attribute directive compartment resolves to an attribute or attribute template when processed, and each statement in an operation directive compartment resolves to an operation or operation template when processed. Figure 2.5 (b) shows a transformation schema that illustrates the following:

1. A name directive compartment may contain source directives and explicit and implicit new directives.

2. An attribute directive compartment may contain explicit and implicit new directives, redefine directives, exclude directives and source directives.

3. An operation directive compartment may contain explicit and implicit new directives, redefine directives, exclude directives and source directives. Source directives and redefine directives in an operation directive compartment may contain embedded exclude and new directives.

2.5. Class Model Transformation – Illustrative Example

This section describes the transformation of a platform-independent server distribution class model into a CORBA distribution model. Server distribution is the process of making a server object available to remote clients. An object is available when clients can communicate with it using remote method invocation. In CORBA, distribution can be realized by: (1) initializing an object request broker (ORB) through which clients communicate with the server, (2) initializing a portable object adapter that is used to manage object properties (e.g., object persistence) and to invoke operations on objects on behalf of the ORB and (3) registering the server with the CORBA naming service.

2.5.1. Server Distribution Aspect Class Model

Figure 2.6 shows a class diagram template of middleware service distribution. The model has six parts. The *Server* class template represents the service to be distributed. It has an associated provided interface represented by *ServerInterface*. The *ServerPreparation* classifier template represents a protocol for preparing the server for distribution. This is accomplished using instances of the *configure* operation template. The *MiddlewarePreparation* classifier template represents a protocol for preparing the middleware features that support distribution, for example, initialization of the CORBA ORB. Tasks associated with preparing the middleware services is accomplished using instances of the *configure* operation template of the *MiddlewarePreparation* classifier template. The *Server* is made available to clients by registering the *Server* with the middleware using instances of the *register* operation template of the *ServiceRegistration* classifier template. After a service has registered, it may be necessary to interact with the middleware registration service, for example, to change a property associated with the server or to reset a property associated with the middleware distribution service. This is accomplished using the *ManageServer* classifier template and instances of its *getProperty* and *setProperty* operation templates.

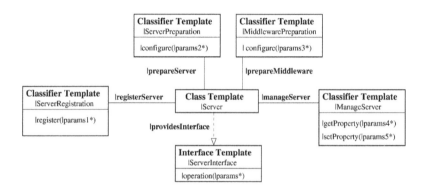

Figure 2.6. *Source Class Distribution Aspect*

2.5.2. CORBA Distribution Class Diagram Transformation Schema

The mappings to transform the generic distribution aspect class model into a CORBA distribution model is specified as a transformation schema as shown in Figure 2.7. The transformation schema has the following features:

1. The preparation of the middleware infrastructure to support server distribution that is represented in the source aspect model by the MiddlewarePreparation classifier template is represented in the transformation schema by the following model elements:

    -   The   source.|MiddlewarePreparation   {name=ORB} transformation schema class represents the CORBA object request broker (ORB).

    -   The   source.|MiddlewarePreparation   {name=POAManager} transformation   schema   interface   and   the   source. |MiddlewarePreparation   {name=POAHelper}   transformation schema class represent parts of the CORBA POA that are used to support   preparation   of   the   middleware   infrastructure. POAHelper provides the narrow operation that is used to provide a reference to the POA while the POAManager provides the activate operation that is used to change the state of the POA manager to active and cause associated POAs to start processing requests.

- The CORBA POA is used to support both preparation of the middleware infrastructure and preparation of the server for distribution. The POA is represented in the transformation schema by the source.|MiddlewarePreparation {name=POA} source.|ServerPreparation transformation schema interface. This model element has two transformation schema operations: |MiddlewarePreparation.| configure name=the_POAManager} (exclude <params>): |POAManager is used to provide a POA manager while the other operation template: |ServerPreparation.| configure {name= servant_to_ reference} (|params2* {name=sobj: |Server}): |CORBA.Object, is used to prepare the server for distribution by converting a server object into a CORBA object reference.

2. The registration of the server with the CORBA distribution service that is represented in the source aspect model by the ServerRegistration classifier template is represented in the transformation schema by three model elements:

- The source.|ServerRegistration {name=NamingContextExtHelper} transformation schema class.

- The source.|ServerRegistration {name=NamingContextExt} transformation schema interface.

- The source.|ServerRegistration {name=NamingComponent} transformation schema class.

3. Facilities for interacting with the CORBA distribution service after the server has been distributed are represented in the source aspect model by the |ManageServer classifier template. In the transformation schema this facility is represented by the |ManageServer{name=Naming} transformation schema class. This class contains two instances of the getProperty operation template and two instances of the setProperty operation template. The Naming class is a part of the CORBA naming service.

4. CORBA requires the creation of an IDL interface file for the server. An IDL interface is similar to a Java interface but may also contain attributes and exceptions. The source.|ServerInterface{name= |IDLInterfaceOperations} transformation schema interface represents a Java interface generated from the IDL interface by the CORBA IDL

compiler. The |IDLInterfacePOA transformation schema class represents a Java class also generated from the IDL interface by the CORBA IDL compiler.

5. The `source.|Server` transformation schema class represents the server to be distributed.

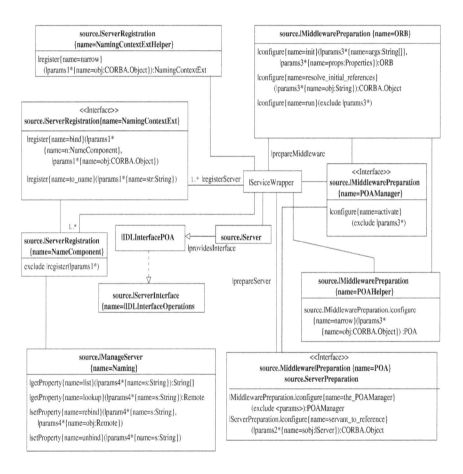

Figure 2.7. *CORBA Class Transformation Schema*

2.5.3. *Processing Transformation Directives*

We have developed an algorithm for systematically processing transformation directives based on the metamodel shown in Figure 2.8. The metamodel describes the static and behavioral properties needed to support class model transformation.

`Source` and `redefine` directives are processed by merging the source aspect model element with the transformation schema model element. A `rename` directive: *ModelElement {name=modelElementName}* is processed by replacing the entire directive by `modelElementName`. An exclude directive, `exclude ModelElement` is processed by eliminating `ModelElement` from its namespace. Implicit `new` directives are processed by removing the word *'new'* from the directive. Explicit `new` directives are processed by adding the model element to the target namespace.

Using these transformation rules, the directives embedded in the transformation schema shown in Figure 2.7 are processed. The resulting CORBA distribution class model is shown in Figure 2.7. This model can be instantiated by supplying values for the templates.

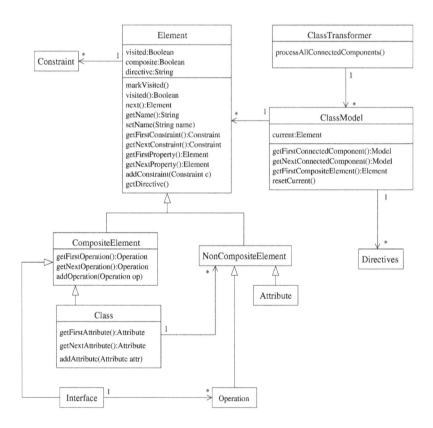

Figure 2.8. *Transformation metamodel for class diagrams*

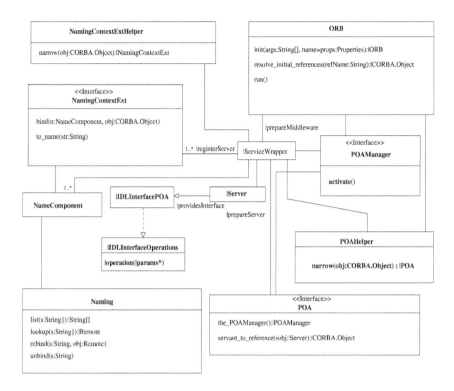

Figure 2.9. *CORBA Distribution Target Aspect Model*

2.6. Discussion and Conclusion

2.6.1. *Model Transformation Using QVT*

QVT transformation specifications are metamodel based, and thus, to specify transformations, the source and target metamodels are needed. In QVT, models are specified using UML 2.0 standard [Obj 03c]. QVT includes a graphical language and a semantically equivalent textual language.

Figure 2.10 illustrates a graphical QVT mapping for transforming a UML interaction model to a class model. Each QVT mapping consists of a source model that is a metamodel description of the model to be transformed and a target model that describes the transformed model. In Figure 2.10, the first mapping is specified as: `Interaction2Class(i:Interaction,c1, c2:Class`. This is a specification of a relation between a source interaction model and a target class model. The relation specifies that each pair of lifelines in the input interaction model (the model to be transformed) that have a message between them will be transformed into a class model consisting of two classes with an association between the classes. The classes will have names corresponding to the types of the lifelines. For example, for ci1:Class is given the same name as the type of the 11:lifeline using the expression, name=11t.name where 11t is the type of the 11 lifeline.

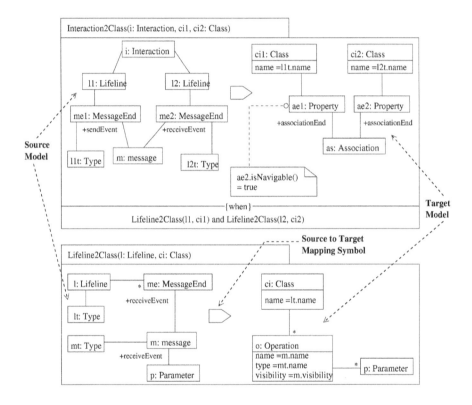

Figure 2.10. *Interaction Diagram to Class Mapping*

The QVT standard also allows dependencies between mappings to be specified using the when and where clauses. Each when clause is a list of mappings that must be accomplished for the relation to which the when clause is specified to hold. In the example the when clause is specified as: when Lifeline2Class(l1,ci1) and Lifeline2Class(l2,ci2). The clause is used in this example to add an operation to a class for each receiveEvent messageEnd.

There are several challenges to specifying transformations using QVT. The UML metamodel for classes and interactions as specified in the UML 2 is fragmented, and the fragments are tied together via several other metamodel packages. As a result, using the UML metamodel to specify transformations can be a difficult process as navigating the UML metamodel may be time consuming and tedious.

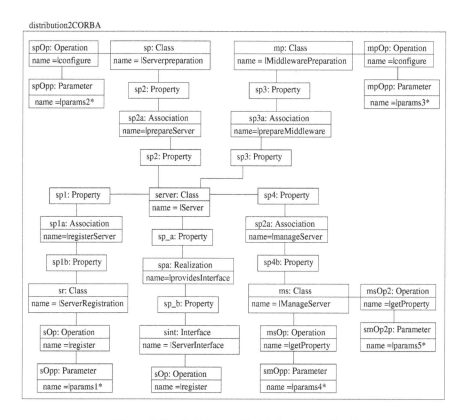

Figure 2.11. *QVT Source Model For Server Distribution*

A second difficulty with specifying model transformations using QVT is the lack of conciseness and legibility of QVT models. Figure 2.11 shows the source model for the QVT mapping corresponding to the source aspect distribution model in Figure 2.6. As can be seen from the model, the QVT specification has 33 composite model elements compared with only six composite model elements in Figure 2.6.

The problem becomes more apparent when the QVT target model for the transformation specified in the transformation schema is examined. Figure 2.12 shows the QVT mapping for |ServiceWrapper, ORB, POAManager, POAHelper, POA and |Server, only six of the twelve composite model elements required in the target model. Compared with the transformation schema with its twelve composite model elements shown in Figure 2.7, the QVT model has forty five composite model elements, and that for only six of the model elements in the transformation schema. A second QVT model for the other models elements may be specified, or the other model elements may be added to the already cluttered model shown in Figure 2.12. The point being underscored here is this: *because QVT is based on the use of the UML metaclasses, the specification of transformations is cumbersome, verbose and difficult to read.* In contrast, the use of transformation schemas is based on the UML instances of metaclasses and a small set of transformation directives. As such, we believe the use of transformation schemas can simplify mappings and enhance the conciseness and readability of specifications.

This chapter presents a new approach to transforming platform-independent design models into platform-specific design models. The approach embeds transformation directives in design models and defines a systematic approach for processing the embedded directives. In addition to research into the consistency of transformations, the model transformation research presented in this article can be extended by applying the technique to other middleware features such as security, reliability and quality of service, and to other middleware such as EJB and .Net.

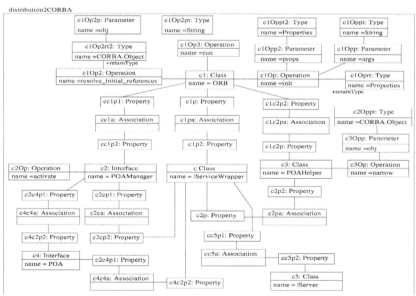

Figure 2.12. *Part Of The QVT Target Model For Server Distribution*

2.7. References

[BAN 04]   BANIASSAD E.CLARKE S., Theme: An Approach for Aspect-Oriented Analysis and Design, *Proceedings of the International Conference on Software Engineering*, 158–167, 2004.

[ISO]   ISO/IEC 10746: BASIC REFERENCE MODEL FOR OPEN DISTRIBUTED PROCESSING, 1995.

[Obj 03b]   OBJECT MANAGEMENT GROUP, The Model Driven Architecture, *URL* http://0ex www.0ex omg.0ex org/0ex mda/, 2003.

[Obj 03c]   OBJECT MANAGEMENT GROUP, The Unified Modeling Language (UML), Version 2.0, URL: http://www.uml.org/, August 2003.

[SCH 02]   SCHMIDT D. C., GOKHALE A., NATARAJAN B., NEEMA S., BAPTY T., PARSONS J., NECHIPURENKO A., GRAY J.WANG N., CoSMIC: A MDA tool for Component Middleware-based Distributed Real-time and Embedded Applications, *Proc. OOPSLA Workshop on Generative Techniques for Model-Driven Architecture*, Seattle, WA USA, November 2002.

[SEL 03]   SELIC B., The Pragmatics of Model-Driven Development, *IEEE Softw.*, 20, 5, 19–25, IEEE Computer Society Press, 2003.

[SIL 04]   SILAGHI R., FONDEMENT F.STROHMEIER A., Towards an MDA-Oriented UML Profile for Distribution, *Proceedings of the 8th IEEE International Enterprise Distributed Object Computing Conference, EDOC*, Monterey, CA, USA, September 2004.

[SIM 05]   SIMMONDS D., SOLBERG A., REDDY R., FRANCE R.GHOSH S., An Aspect Oriented Model Driven Framework, *Proceedings of the Ninth IEEE "The Enterprise Computing Conference" (EDOC 2005)*, Enschede, Netherlands, IEEE Computer Society Press, 119-130, September 2005.

[The 05]   THE OBJECT MANAGEMENT GROUP, MOF QVT Final Adopted Specification, , OMG, ptc/05-11-01, 2005.

[WAD 02]   WADSACK J. P.JAHNKE J. H., Towards Model-Driven Middleware Maintenance, *Proc. OOPSLA 2002 Workshop Generative Techniques in the context of Model Driven Architecture*, France, 2002.

CHAPTER 3

Rationale of the UML profile for Marte[1]

Chapter written by Sébastien Gérard and Huascar Espinoza

CEA-List/DRT/DTSI/SOL/LLSP
91191 Gif-sur-Yvette cedex
{Sebastien.Gerard, Huascar.Espinoza}@cea.fr

3.1. Introduction

Since the adoption of the UML standard and its new advanced release UML2, this modeling language has been used for development of a large number of time-critical and resource-critical systems. Based on this experience, a consensus has emerged that, while a useful tool, UML is lacking in some key areas that are of particular concern to real-time and embedded system designers and developers. In particular, it was noticed that first the lack of quantifiable notions of time and resources was an impediment to its broader use in the real-time and embedded domain. Second, the need for rigorous semantics definition is also a mandatory requirement for a widespread usage of the UML for RT/E systems development. And third, specific constructs were required to build models using artifacts related the real-time operating system level such as task and semaphore.

Fortunately, and contrary to an often expressed opinion, it was discovered that UML had all the requisite mechanisms for addressing these issues, in particular through its extensibility facilities. This made the job much easier, since it was unnecessary to add new fundamental modeling concepts to UML

---

[1] At the time this chapter has been written, all the work related to Marte was still ongoing work. The final version of the Marte standard is expected to be available in December 2006.

– so-called "heavyweight" extensions. Consequently, the job consisted of defining a standard way of using these capabilities to represent concepts and practices from the real-time and embedded domain.

Hence, this specification of a UML™ profile adds capabilities on the one hand for modeling Real Time and Embedded Systems (RTES), and on the other hand for analyzing schedulability and performance properties of UML specifications. This new profile is intended to replace the existing UML Profile for Schedulability, Performance and Time [OMG 05b]. This extension, called the Marte profile, should address specification, design, and verification stages of the development cycle of RTES. It wants to address the two branches of the V cycle, i.e. modeling and validation and verification. Modeling capabilities have to ensure both hardware and software aspects of RTES in order to improve communication/exchange between developers. It also has to foster the construction of models that may be used to make quantitative analysis regarding hardware and software characteristics. Finally, it should enable interoperability between developments tools used all along the development process.

Regarding the OMG standard process, the specification of a new standard specification follows the publication of what is called a request for proposal (RFP) that deals with a list of requirements the new standard will have to comply with. Following this process, Marte is then response to the following RFP: UML PROFILE FOR MODELING AND ANALYSIS OF REAL-TIME AND EMBEDDED SYSTEMS (MARTE) RFP [OMG 05a]. Driven by these requirements, the main guiding principles used to write the Marte specification have been:

— the profile should support independent modeling of both software or hardware parts of RT/E systems and the relationships between them;

— the profile has to provide modeling constructs covering the development process of RT/E systems. Such features may be categorized into qualitative (parallelism, synchronization, communication) or quantitative (deadline, periodicity). The profile must provide high-level modeling constructs for specification purpose, for example, but also low-level construct for implementation purpose;

— as much as possible, modelers should not be hindered in the way they use UML to represent their systems just to be able to do model analysis. That is, rather than enforcing a specific approach or modeling style for real-time systems, the profile should allow modelers to choose the style and modeling constructs that they feel are the best fit to their needs at that time;

— modelers should be able to take advantage of different types of model analysis techniques without requiring a deep understanding of the inner workings of those techniques. The steep learning curve behind many of the current model analysis methods has been one of the major impediments to their adoption;

– the profile must support all the current mainstream real-time technologies, design paradigms, and model analysis techniques. However, it should also be fully open to new developments in all of these areas;

– it must foster to construct UML models that can be used to make quantitative and partitioning predictions and analysis regarding hardware and software characteristics of the RT/E system. In particular, it is important to be able to perform such analyses early in the development cycle. For that, it has to be possible to analyze partial models. It should be possible to automatically construct different analysis-specific models directly from a given UML model. Such tools should be able to read the model, process it, and feed the results back to the modeler in terms of the original UML model.

The Marte specification is a result of common work done by a consortium of OMG members: ProMarte[2]. The following companies submitted and/or supported parts of this specification: Alcatel, ARTISAN Software Tools, Carleton University, Commissariat à l'Energie Atomique, ESEO, ENSIETA, International Business Machines, I-Logix, INRIA, Lockheed Martin, Mentor Graphics Corporation, Software Engineering Institute (Carnegie Mellon University), Softeam, Telelogic AB, Thales and Tri-Pacific Software.

3.2. Outlines of Marte

3.2.1. *Marte and other OMG standards related RT/E*

The Marte profile replaces the current profile for Schedulability, Performance, and Time [OMG 05b]. The definition of Marte relies on a set of generic (i.e. not specific to RT/E) existing OMG specifications (Figure 3.1). The most obvious of these is the UML 2 Superstructure specification, which is the basis for any UML profile[3]. It also uses the OCL 2.0 specification for all constraints specified in OCL. In addition, it uses the MOF 2.0 Queries, Views, and Transformation framework to define any model transformation rules (e.g., rules for transforming a MARTE stereotype into a corresponding analysis model element).

In addition to previous generic OMG specifications, Marte is also related to other OMG specifications which concern is the RT/E domain:

– The UML profile for Modeling Quality of Service and Fault Tolerance Characteristics and Mechanisms [OMG 04]. This specification provides, among other things, a generic metamodel for defining different qualities of service;

---

[2] www.promarte.org

[3] Note that the Superstructure is dependent on UML compliance level 3 (L3), which is the complete UML metamodel.

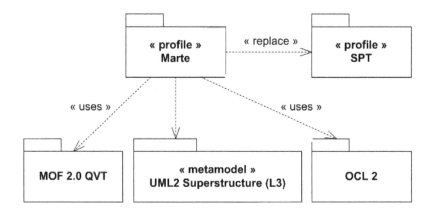

Figure 3.1. *Informal description of the Marte dependencies with other OMG standards*

— The UML profile for Systems Engineering [OMG 06]. This one deals with many of the same areas, such as the modeling of platforms and their constituent elements (hardware resources) and the allocation of software to platforms (i.e., deployment). In areas where there is conceptual overlap, MARTE either reuses the corresponding SysML stereotypes, or defines elements that are conceptually and terminologically aligned with SysML;

— The Executable UML Foundation specification (currently in progress) defines, among other things, a model of causality for UML that is at the core of various scenario-based analysis methods (such as performance and schedulability analyses). The MARTE causality model must be fully consistent with the model specified in the Executable UML Foundation spec;

— The Real-Time CORBA specification is used to provide both an example of how the MARTE profile is applied and a reusable asset that can be utilized in UML models that incorporate Real-Time CORBA.

3.2.2. *A foundation for model driven techniques*

The profile definition subscribes to the MDA approach promoted by OMG putting in the center of the development process of RTE systems the model artifact. Hence, it is intended to provide a foundation for applying transformations from UML models into a wide variety of model transformations, as for example to couple modeling tools with specific analysis tools such as schedulability analysis tools. A typical environment build for exploiting the profile would consist of a set of tools, including tools from one of the three following categories: modeling tools, model transformers or analysis tools.

The schema of Figure 3.2 describes an example of such environment architecture (prototypes of such tool chains have been already produced based on SPT). The left side of the picture illustrates the fact that a modeler is first able to describe a model of its application thanks to modeling artifacts provided by Marte. Second the modeler may also add additional information to its model by annotations (specific stereotypes) in order to for example provide the required semantics required for performing a special kind of analysis or a dedicated code generation. The right side of the picture illustrates the ability of external tools (external means non-UML based tool) to perform specific action and produce results (e.g. a schedulability analysis or a code generation). The middle part of the picture illustrates the connection of UML-tools and non-UML tools. The forward path shows the way the UML model is expected to be transformed to a format readable by an analysis tool. The dashed line indicates a potential feedback path to re-import the analysis results into the UML diagrams.

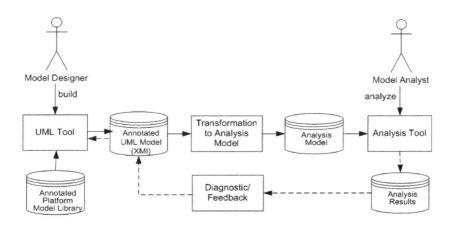

Figure 3.2. *A Tool Chain for Carrying out Analysis of a Model*

3.2.3. *How should the specification be used?*

This section aims to describe which potential actors may use this specification and how they can do it. Of course, neither the actors nor use cases described in this section represent an exclusive set for how this specification can be used, but rather reflect some of the ways that we expect it to be used or (in most cases) expanded.

3.2.3.1. *Expected users*

Figure 3.3 describes a set of potential actors that may use this specification for designing RT/E systems.

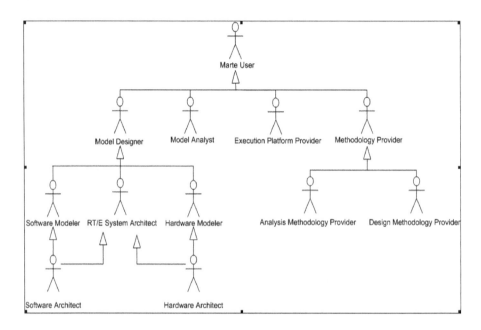

Figure 3.3. *Possible taxonomy of actors using the Marte specification*

— *Model Designer:* These are modelers that design models dedicated to be applied in the context of the development process of RT/E systems. Models may be used for usual specification, design or implementation stages, but they may be also used for analyzing in order to determine whether they will meet their performance and schedulability requirements:

- *RT/E Systems Architect:* These are specific modelers concerned with the overall architecture and they usually make trade-offs between implementing functionality in hardware, software, or both;

- *Hardware Modeler:* These are modelers specifically dedicated to hardware aspects of the RT/E systems development;

- *Hardware Architect:* These are modelers concerned by designing hardware architecture;

- *Software Modeler:* These are modelers specifically dedicated to software aspects of the RT/E systems development;

- *Software Architect:* These are modelers concerned with designing software architecture;

— *Model Analyst:* These are modelers concerned with annotating system models in order to perform specific analysis methodologies;

— *Execution Platform Provider*: These are developers and vendors of run-time technologies (hardware- or/and software-based platforms) such as Real-Time CORBA, real-time operating systems and specific hardware components;

— *Methodology Provider:* These are the individuals and teams who are responsible for defining model-based methodology for RT/E domain. This category includes UML tool providers:

- *Design Methodology Provider:* These are specialized methodology providers who are responsible for defining model-based methodology for specifying, designing or/and implementing RT/E systems;

- *Analysis Methodology Provider:* These are specialized methodology providers who are responsible for defining model-based analysis methodology such as RMA or queuing theory, as well as technology provider such as tool vendors providing tools and processes for supporting particular model analysis methods.

3.2.3.2. Marte common use cases

According to the previous actor taxonomy, it is expected that the Marte specification will be use at least following some predefined use cases. Common possible usages of the Marte profile are specified in the use case diagram depicted in Figure 3.4.

— Details of the use case "build Model"
- *Actor:* Modeler
- *Description:* A modeler builds a model iterating it through several stages defined in an appropriate development process. According to a given methodology (see the "define Methodology" use case), a modeler uses appropriate UML extensions or specific model libraries defined in the Marte specification in order to describe the RT/E aspects in the model of their system.
- *Deliverable:* The result of this use case is a model of the user system containing all its RT/E specificities.

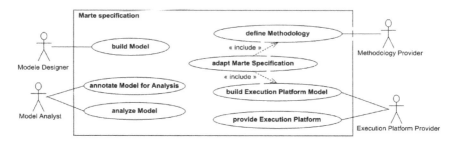

Figure 3.4. *Common use cases of the Marte specification*

— Details of the use case "adapt Marte Specification"

- *Actor:* Methodology Provider and Execution Platform Provider;

- *Description:* This use case consists of defining a specific Marte sub-profile. The motivations to adapt Marte may be either to deal with a specific domain not covered by Marte or to define restrictions on the usage of Marte modeling constructs. In the former case, the actor may either specialize Marte modeling constructs in order to adapt them suitably to their needs or introduce new concepts not available in Marte. The second way to adapt the Marte specification is to define modeling rules in order to constraint the usage of the specification;

- *Deliverable:* The outcome of this use case is a definition of Marte extension that takes the form a UML profile based on the Marte specification. The dependencies with the Marte profile may be merge import or specialization.

— Details of the use case "define Methodology"

- *Actor:* Methodology Provider;

- *Description:* This use case consists of defining how to use the Marte specification for a given purpose. For example, one may define a specific methodology for the design of electronic automotive systems (cf. the EAST-ADL appendix) or for avionics (see AADL appendix). One may also define model-based analysis methodology such as schedulability or performance analysis;

- *Deliverable:* The outcome of this use case is a model-based methodology. This latter may include a process description, a set of constraint rules and a set of required techniques that applies to the methodology. If necessary, this use case may also include the definition of an extension of the Marte profile (include of the "extend Marte Specification" use case).

— Details of the use case "annotate Model for Analysis"

- *Actor:* Model Analyst;

- *Description:* The model analyst uses appropriate Marte extensions, as defined for example in a specific analysis methodology, in order to appropriately annotate models in order to perform a given analysis techniques;

- *Deliverable:* The outcome of this use case is a model annotated with Marte extensions and ready for performing specific analysis;

— Details of the use case "analyze Model"

- *Actor:* Model Analyst;

- *Description:* The model analyst perform a given analysis techniques on a model. The purpose of the analysis may be varied depending of the nature of the analysis techniques used. Some examples of analysis are: schedulability or performance analyses;

- *Deliverable:* The outcomes of this use case are analysis results.

— Details of the use case "build Execution Platform Model"

- *Actor:* Execution Platform Provider;

- *Description:* This use case consists of building model of execution platform for Marte based developments of RT/E systems;

- *Deliverable:* The outcome of this use case is a Marte compatible execution platform model.

— Details of the use case "provide Execution Platform"

- *Actor:* Execution Platform Provider;

- *Description:* This use case consists of providing execution platform conform to a given model of platform;

- *Deliverable:* The outcome of this use case is an execution platform.

3.3. Profile architecture

The Marte profile architecture model consists of three main packages:

— The Time and Concurrent Resource Modeling package (TCRM); it defines basic model constructs for time and resource, especially concurrent resources. This foundational concepts are then refined in both following package in order to fit with both modeling and analyzing concerns;

— The RealTime and Embedded application Modeling package (RTEAM); it enables modeling of RT/E application. It concerns mainly defining on the one hand high-level model constructs to depict real-time and embedded features of application, and on the other hand to enable the description of execution platforms, software as well as hardware;

— The RealTime and Embedded application Analysis; it provides a generic support for analyzing annotated models. This generic framework is also refined in order to cope with schedulability and performance analysis. It is also expected that the generic framework for analysis will be specialized/extended to support other kind of quantitative analysis, such as power consumption, memory use or reliability.

3.4. References

[OMG 04]   Object Management Group, UML Profile for Modeling Quality of Service
             and Fault Tolerance Characteristics and Mechanisms, ptc/04-09-01, 2004.

[OMG 05a]   Object Management Group, UML Profile for Modeling and Analysis of
             Real-Time and Embedded systems (MARTE) RFP, realtime/05-02-06, 2005.

[OMG 05b]   Object Management Group, UML Profile for Schedulability, Performance
             and Time, Version 1.1., formal/05-01-02, 2005.

[OMG 06]   Object Management Group, Systems Modeling Language (SysML) Specification,
             ptc/06-05-04, 2006.

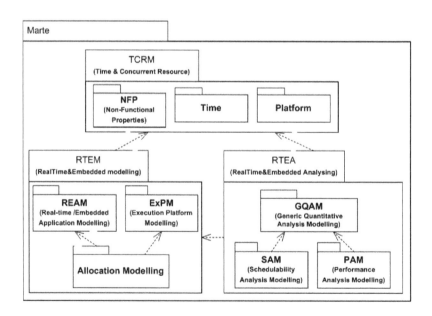

Figure 3.5. *Architecture of the Marte profile*

CHAPTER 4

From UML to Performance Analysis Models by Abstraction-raising Transformation

Chapter written by Dorina Petriu and Antonino Sabetta

Department of Systems and Computer Engineering
Carleton University, Ottawa (Ontario) Canada
{petriu@sce.carleton.ca; sabetta}@acm.org

4.1. Introduction

The change of focus from code to models promoted by OMG's Model Driven Architecture (MDA) [OMG 03] raises the need for formal verification of non-functional characteristics of UML software models, such as performance, reliability, scalability, security, etc. Over the years, many modeling formalisms (e.g., queueing networks, Petri nets, fault trees, formal logic, process algebras, etc.) and corresponding tools have been developed for the analysis of different non-functional properties. Now the challenge is not to reinvent new analysis methods targeted to UML models, but to bridge the gap between UML-based software development tools and different existing analysis formalisms and tools.

In general, an analysis model abstracts away many details of the original software model, emphasizing only aspects of interests for the respective analysis. A transformation whereby a more abstract target analysis model is generated from a source software model is called "abstraction-raising" transformation [SAB 05], as opposed to a "refining" transformation that produces a more detailed target model. According to the taxonomy of model transformations proposed in [MEN 05], the abstraction-raising transformation discussed in this chapter is both exogenous (i.e., the source and target models are different) and vertical (the abstraction level is different).

Traditionally, analysis models were built "by hand" by specialists in the field, who "abstracted" from the software only the properties of interests. However, in the context of MDA, a new approach for constructing analysis models is emerging, where software models are automatically transformed into different analysis models. For example, a formal logic model for analysing security characteristics is obtained automatically from UML in [JUR 04]. Transformations from UML into different performance models have been surveyed in [BAL 04]. Examples of such transformations are from UML to Layered Queueing Networks in [PET 02] [PET 03], to Stochastic Petri Nets in [BER 02], and to Stochastic Process Algebra in [CAV 04]. More recently, a transformation framework from multiple design models into different performance models was proposed in [WOO 05]. A considerable challenge is to bridge the semantic gap between the UML source model and a target model which represents more abstract concepts.

Different kinds of analysis techniques may require additional annotations to the UML model to express, for instance, non-functional requirements and characteristics, or the user's directives for the desired analysis. OMG's solution to this problem is to define standard UML profiles for different purposes. Examples of such profiles are the *UML Profile for Schedulability, Performance, and Time* (SPT) [OMG 05a] and *UML Profile for Modeling and Analysis of Real-Time and Embedded systems* (MARTE) [OMG 05c], which will upgrade SPT to UML 2.0 and extend its scope with modeling capabilities for real-time and embedded systems.

The abstraction-raising transformation concept used in this chapter was first proposed by the authors in [SAB 05], where it was applied to the transformation from UML to Klaper (Kernel LAnguage for PErformance and Reliability analysis of component-based systems) [GRA 05]. Here the work from [SAB 05] is extended as follows: a) it explains more clearly the goals of the two steps (i.e., abstraction-raising and mapping), which are kept decoupled; b) it presents a graph-grammar based solution to the challenging problem of extending the source model with analysis-specific concepts, while keeping the input UML (meta)model intact, and c) it proposes a QVT-based approach for the mapping step. The whole approach is illustrated by a transformation from UML annotated with SPT to Layered Queueing Networks (LQN) [ROL 95] [WOO 95].

The chapter is organized as follows: the next section describes the conceptual approach for the abstraction-raising transformation, section 4.3 presents the source and target model and their mapping, section 4.4 describes the realization of the two steps for the UML-to-LQN transformation, section 4.5 describes its application to a case study and section 4.6 gives the conclusions.

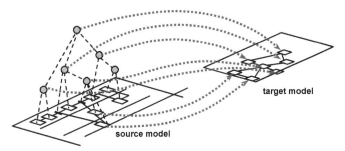

Figure 4.1. *Principle of abstraction-raising transformation*

4.2. Conceptual Approach for Abstraction-raising Transformation

The proposed approach combines two concepts that, so far, have been used separately in model transformations: relational and graph grammar-based transformations [CZA 03]. In the relational approach, which is used in the QVT standard [OMG 05b], the source and target model are described each by its own metamodel; a transformation defines relations (mappings) between different element types of the source and target (meta)models. According to [OMG 05b], a *Transformation* is a generalization of both *Relation* and *Mapping*. Relations are bi-directional transformation specifications, whereas Mappings are unidirectional transformation implementations.

On the other hand, the graph transformation approach specifies how elements of one model are transformed into elements of another model in an operational manner, by using a set of transformation rules. The graph-transformation and relational approaches are compared in [KUS 04]. While the former is based on matching and replacement, the latter is based on matching and reconciliation. The conclusion is that, in spite of their differences, advantages and disadvantages, the two approaches are rather similar. More research is needed to identify which one is more suitable for certain kinds of applications.

In the approach followed in this chapter (illustrated in Figure 4.1), we keep the idea that the source and target models are described by separate metamodels, between which transformations must be defined. However, in our case the target metamodel represents analysis domain concepts, which are usually at a higher-level of abstraction than the source model concepts. In order to define mappings between the source and target models, sometimes it is necessary to group (aggregate) a large number of source model elements according to certain rules, and to map the whole group to a single target element.

The aggregation rules correspond to the raising in the abstraction level, necessary to bridge the semantic gap between the source and target model. Such rules are dependent on the semantic differences between the source and target model, and are *not* represented in the source metamodel. Therefore, a new mechanism is needed to express the aggregation rules, in addition to the mechanism for defining the transformation from the source to the target model.

We propose to use a graph grammar [ROZ 97] for describing the aggregation rules; the terminals of the graph grammar correspond to meta-objects from the source model, whereas the non-terminals correspond to more abstract concepts that will be transformed *directly* into target model concepts. Some target model elements can be obtained by a direct mapping from source models elements, like in a relational transformation, whereas other target elements, representing more abstract concepts, correspond to graph-grammar non-terminals obtained by parsing the source model.

To sum up, two distinct problems arise in the transformation from design models to analysis models. The first is the need to identify more expressive and meaningful abstractions in the source model; the second is the need to define clear and manageable mapping rules from the source to the target domain. We argue that these two concerns have very specific characteristics and thus must be decoupled in order to address them more effectively with specialized approaches.

Another important goal of the proposed abstraction-raising approach is to keep the original UML model intact. Any extension of the source model with domain-specific concepts with the purpose to facilitate the transformation to the target model is recorded only in the graph grammar expressing the aggregation rules and does not affect the UML (meta)model. We propose to separate the concern of parsing the source UML model for extracting higher-level of abstraction concepts from the mapping to the target model, as shown in Figure 4.2. The latter could then be realized by standard MDA techniques by using QVT-like languages.

4.3. Two-step abstraction-raising transformation

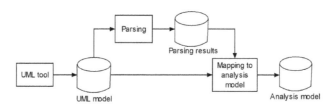

Figure 4.2. *The proposed approach in the context of a typical model transformation chain*

The proposed approach is illustrated with a transformation from UML models with SPT [OMG 05a] annotations (i.e., UML+SPT) to LQN performance models. A simple case study is presented in this section: an e-commerce application designed as a client/server system with three basic components: a user interface, an e-commerce server and a database (see the components and their allocation to hardware devices in Figure 4.3). For the sake of conciseness, we will consider a single specific usage scenario, the check-out procedure, represented by the activity diagram from Figure 4.3. After the user has selected one or more items, the first client–server interaction takes place, with the UserInterface component acting as a client of the ECommServ component, which in turn behaves as a client to the DBMS server in another client-server interaction.

4.3.1. *Description of the Source Model*

We assume that the source UML model describes the high-level software architecture and deployment to hardware devices, as component/deployment diagram(s), while the key scenario(s) for performance analysis are expressed as activity diagram(s), as in Figure 4.3. We also assume that all the information required for the generation of the analysis model is available from the source UML model, possibly by means of suitable annotations in compliance with one or more profiles. In our example, SPT [OMG 05a] is used for performance annotations.

The SPT Profile contains a Performance sub-profile that identifies the main basic abstractions used in performance analysis. Scenarios define response paths through the system, and can have QoS requirements such as response times or throughputs. Each scenario is executed by a workload, which can be closed or open, and has the usual characteristics (number of clients or arrival rate, etc.). Scenarios are composed of scenario steps that can be joined in sequences, loops, branches, fork/joins, etc.

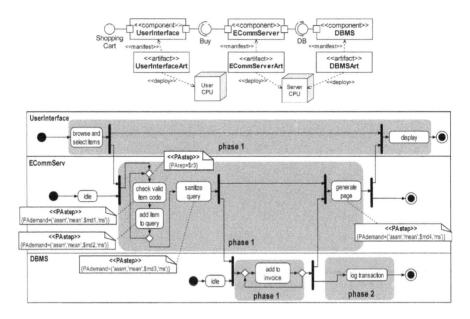

Figure 4.3. *Source model example*

A scenario step may be an elementary operation at the lowest level of granularity, or a complex sub-scenario. Each step has a mean number of repetitions, a host execution demand, other demand to resources and its own QoS characteristics. Resources are another basic abstraction, and can be active or passive, each with their own attributes.

A more detailed description of the Performance sub-profile and its application is given in [PET 02]. Not all SPT annotations are shown in Figure 4.3, just a few *PAStep* stereotypes applied to different activities. The tagged value PAdemand gives the CPU demand for a step. For instance, *PAdemand ={'assm', 'mean', $md1, 'ms'}* means that the step needs to execute in average *$md1* miliseconds, and that this is an *assumed* demand (as opposed to *measured*). The tagged value *PArep = $r* gives the average number of loop repetitions. Such quantitative annotations will be used during the transformation process to compute the parameter of the target performance model, as discussed later in section 4.4.3.

4.3.2. Description of the Target Model

LQN was developed as an extension of the well-known Queueing Network model [ROL 95] [WOO 95]. A LQN model is an acyclic graph, with nodes representing software entities and hardware devices, and arcs denoting service requests (see Figure 4.10). The software entities also known as *tasks* are drawn as parallelograms, and the hardware devices as circles. Each kind of service offered by a LQN task is modeled as a so-called *entry*, drawn as a smaller parallelogram. Every entry may be decomposed in two sequential *phases* of service: during *phase1* the client is blocked waiting for the server's reply, which is sent at the end of the phase. The client will continue its execution, and the server will complete its *phase 2* of service in parallel with the client. Every phase has its own execution time demands and requests for other services, represented as arcs to other entries. LQN has more features that are not described here for the sake of simplicity.

4.3.3. *Mapping Approach*

Some of the relations between UML and LQN elements are straightforward, and can be described as one-to-one correspondences between elements of the two metamodels. For instance, each UML *component* is mapped to an LQN *task*, each service offered by a component is mapped to an *entry*, each processing node to a processor, and so on.

However, there are cases where a group of elements in the source model represents, as a whole, an *abstraction* that must be mapped eventually to a single LQN element, as in the case of *phases* of *entries*. For example, the shaded areas from Figure 4.3 group together activities that correspond, as a whole group, to different phases of service of different entries. Therefore, a technique is needed to identify and to represent explicitly these abstractions, in order to facilitate the definition and application of the transformation rules. This leads to the idea of extending the source model with analysis-specific concepts. However, at the same time we need to keep the UML (meta)model intact. The chapter addresses these two contradictory requirements.

4.4. Two-step abstraction-raising transformation

4.4.1. *Proposed Approach*

The approach proposed in this chapter is structured in two steps. The *first step* uses a graph grammar to parse the activity diagrams from the UML+SPT input model, in order to extract a set of key abstractions that will be mapped onto concepts of the target domain. A "correct" activity diagram input is reduced to the starting symbol *AD* by parsing. In the parsing process, a set of non-terminals is identified and an *Abstract Syntax Tree* (AST) is constructed. In our approach, the AST represents an extension of the input UML+SPT model, and its nodes will be used as a source for relational mappings just like any standard UML objects. At the metamodel level, the types of nodes that appear in AST can be regarded as a set of new metaclasses that are added on top of the standard UML metamodel. They represent concepts that are specific to the target domain and correspond to the more "abstract" constructions found in the source model by parsing.

Figure 4.4 shows a simplified metamodel for UML 2.0 activity diagrams extended with target domain concepts (shaded). The main UML 2.0 metaclasses are: ActivityPartition, ActivityNode and ActivityEdge. ActivityPartition corresponds to a software component participating in a client/server interaction, which is deployed as an Artifact instance on a Device instances stereotyped «PAhost» in the deployment diagram. An ActivityNode models units of executable functionality through the Action specialization, and nodes that coordinate the control flow through the ControlNode specialization. A ControlNode can be further specialized into InitialNode, FinalNode, ForkNode, MergeNode, etc (not shown in Figure 4.4). An ActivityEdge models directed connections between two ActivityNode instances, and represents the flow of control or data in the activity diagram.

The shaded metaclasses from Figure 4.4 can be considered as an extension to the UML metamodel. Instances of these metaclasses will be created by parsing and added to the AST, which represents an extension of the input UML+SPT model. An important requirement when defining such a metamodel extension is to avoid any changes to the original UML metamodel. This ensures the compliance with the UML standard and the compatibility with the available tools. In order to meet such a requirement, the associations between the extension metaclasses (shaded) and the UML metaclasses should be navigable only from the former to the latter and not vice versa, as this would require adding new attributes to UML standard metaclasses.

The *second step* of the proposed approach may use standard relational mapping techniques, such as those based on the QVT standard, to define transformations from the extended model obtained in the first step, to the target analysis model. The extended model (i.e., the input UML+SPT model and the AST obtained by parsing) contains explicitly all the higher-level concepts that need to be mapped to target model elements.

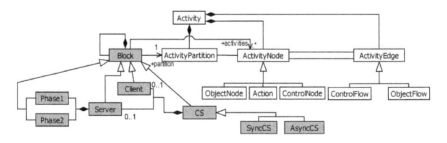

Figure 4.4. *Extended source metamodel*

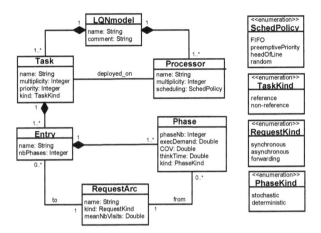

Figure 4.5. *Simplified LQN metamodel*

4.4.2. *Graph Grammar used for Abstraction Raising*

This section presents the graph grammar used to parse the activity diagrams found in a source model. The grammar describes activity diagrams that not only are compliant with the UML 2 specification, but also abide additional well-formedness rules related to the way in which different component interact. This restricts the family of diagrams to those that can be converted into an LQN model. More specifically, the graph-grammar described here is restricted to the client/server communication pattern for the sake of simplicity. The grammar can be extended to other inter-communication patterns for which mappings to LQN exist.

The grammar is defined by the 4-tuple **G={T, N, S, R}** whose elements are:

- Set of terminal symbols **T** = {*Action, Partition, InitialNode, ActivityFinalNode, Fork, Join, ControlFlow, DecisionNode*};

- Set of non-terminals symbols **N** = {*AD, block, seq, loop, cond, phase1, phase2, CS, a-client, s-client, server, client*};

- Starting symbol **S**: *AD*;

- Set of derivation rules **R**: given in Figure 4.5.

The terminal symbols in **T** are a subset of the metaclasses defined in the Activities package that is part of the standard UML2 metamodel specification. The grammar has been devised so that concepts that do not exist in the UML metamodel but that are important in the LQN domain are represented by suitable non-terminal symbols. This implies that the definition of the grammar is specific to the chosen target model.

The grammar rules are applied for reduction as follows: when a sub-graph matching the right hand side (*rhs*) of a rule is found in the host graph (i.e., in the source model possibly rewritten by previous rules), the matching sub-graph is removed and is replaced by the left hand side (*lhs*) of the rule, according to the embedding policy. More precisely: a) the edges attached to *rhs* nodes kept in the *lhs* are preserved (they represent the "context"); b) the edges left dangling (because of the removal of some node from the *lhs*) are removed; c) if a node in the *rhs* is rewritten as one node in the *lhs*, then all the edges attached to the former are redirected to the latter (this applies to non-injective morphisms too).

The graph grammar is structured so that high level constructs as loops,

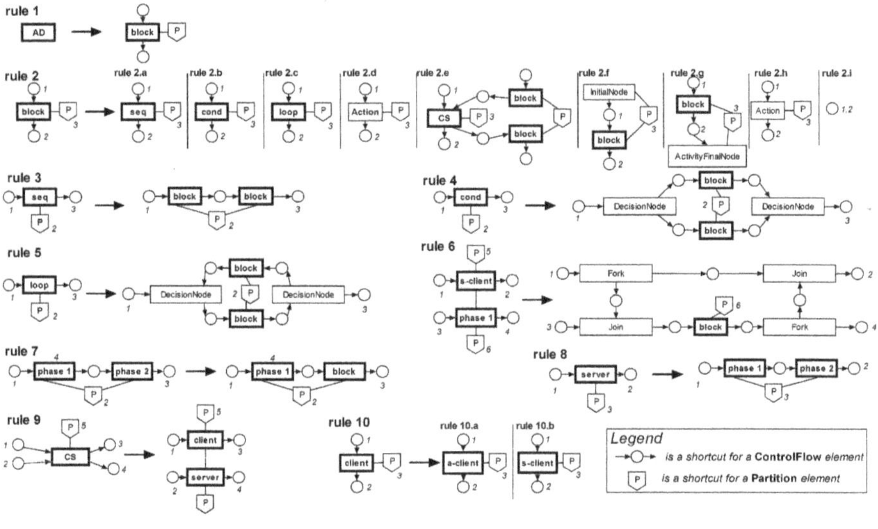

Figure 4.6. *Production rules of the graph grammar for activity diagrams*

conditional structures, sequences, client-server interactions and server phases are discovered through parsing. To this end the concept of a *block* has been introduced and formally defined by rule 2. Several definitions in rule 2 are recursive, which raises the abstraction power of the proposed technique. Basic constructs such as sequences, conditional blocks and loops are defined, in terms of blocks and terminal symbols, by rules 3, 4 and 5. Rule 6 is used to deal with the client-server pattern. Remarkably, the block that represents the behaviour of the server can be as simple as an elementary *action* or as complex as a big block whose structure could contain in turn other client-server interactions and arbitrarily nested conditions, loops and sequences. The abstraction obtained by the application of rule 6 yields a simpler structure where the client and the server parts are clearly identified, and corresponding nodes are inserted into the AST. It is important to observe that the server part obtained by rule 6 is *not* everything the server does to fulfill the client request, but it represents only *phase1* of the server behaviour. Rule 7 states that the second phase is a block that immediately follows a phase 1. Obviously this is one of those cases where the parsing algorithm, i.e. the sequence in which the grammar rules are applied, significantly affects the outcome of the parsing; we assume that this rule is applied only when none of the rules 1 to 6 can be applied. Rule 8 states that a server behaviour is a sequence of a *phase1* and a *phase2* in the same partition. Rule 9 defines, at the highest abstraction level, the client-server pattern, whereas rule 10 allows a client to be either synchronous or asynchronous. A rule analogous to rule 6 defining the asynchronous client-server pattern has been omitted here for space reasons.

4.4.3. *Mapping from the Extended Source Model to LQN*

The parsing of the source model verifies the compliance of the input model with the grammar, and if the verification is successful, an extended source model is generated (which contains the original UML source model plus the AST). The generation of the target LQN model from the extended source model is done in two big steps, A and B, described here in an imperative fashion for convenience:

A. Generating LQN tasks and processors from structural diagrams
- Components or active objects stereotyped «PAresource» are mapped to LQN software tasks (multiplicity is taken into account to generate replicated tasks or multi-servers). Initialize the task attribute "kind=reference";
- Processing nodes stereotyped «PAhost» are mapped to LQN Processor;
- Deployment: the relationship chain «manifest» and «deploy» between a component, a corresponding artifact and a processor is mapped to an LQN request arc between the task representing the component and its processor;
- Non-processing nodes mapped to LQN tasks that represent hardware devices (a dummy processor is also created).

B. Generating LQN entries and phases from scenarios
- Each task has at least an entry, which has at least a phase 1. Reference tasks (those that play exclusively the role of clients) will end up with a default entry and phase. Non-reference tasks (which play the role of server at least once) will have an entry for each client/server interaction they participate in;
- For each scenario:
    - For each CS client/server interaction identified in a scenario, generate the following LQN elements:
        - a server entry that corresponds to the current CS interaction,
        - phase1 and phase2 mapped to its corresponding phases; the service time for each phase as the weighted sum of the «PAdemand» values corresponding

to the activities contained in the phase was computed in the parsing phase and is stored in AST,
- a request arc from the current {client, entry, phase} to {server, entry},
- assign the server's attribute "`kind=non_reference`".

4.5. Application of the proposed transformation

The transformation approach proposed in section 4.4 is applied here to the case study introduced in section 4.3.1. In the abstraction-raising step, the input model is parsed and an extended model is derived from it. In the mapping step, the target LQN model is obtained by a QVT transformation.

4.5.1. *Parsing*

The graph grammar introduced in section 4.4.2 is used to identify occurrences of the client/server interaction pattern and the phases of server-side behaviours. Let us examine the derivation of the LQN model in Figure 4.10 from the source UML model in Figure 4.3. Due to space constraints, we present here only a few parsing steps, but the complete process can be easily reproduced by applying the specified grammar rules.

The diagram in Figure 4.7-A is the result of the following parsing steps applied to the graph representing the source activity diagram.
- All the actions are transformed into blocks (rule 2.h).
- The initial and final nodes are merged with the blocks they are attached to (rules 2.i, 2.f, 2.g).
- All sequences of blocks are transformed into blocks. For instance the sequence composed of the two activities "check valid item code" and "add item to query" become one block (rules 3 and 2.a)
- Loops are reduced to blocks (rules 2.i, 5, 2.c).
- The newly created sequences of blocks (e.g. those deriving by the reduction of loops in the previous step) are reduced to blocks (rules 3 and 2.a).

The client-server interaction involving the e-commerce server and the DBMS component (i.e. the shaded area in 7-A) is then recognized and reduced to the node *c24* in 7-C. In the process, non-terminal symbols are generated (b9, b11, b4 and b14 in Figure 4.7-B', 7-B''and 7-C) that correspond respectively to the computation performed by the server, to that performed by the client and to the overall client-server pattern.

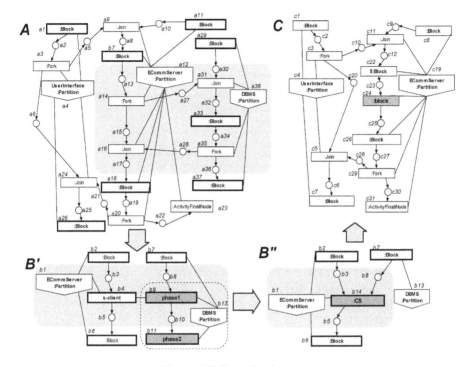

Figure 4.7. *Example of parsing*

In more detail, this is done by applying the following reduction sequence:

- The left hand side of rule 6 matches the shaded area in Figure 4.7-A so the elements b4 and b9 are generated in 7-B';

- Rule 7 is applied so that node a37 (which is a block following a phase 1) is identified as a phase2 (b11 in Figure 4.7-B'). The graph in Figure 4.7-B'' is derived from that of Figure 4.7-B' by using two more rules;

- First, the two phases identified in the previous step are merged to a single server node (not shown in Figure 4.7) by means of rule 8;

- Then, the server node (generated in the previous step) and the client node (b4) are merged by rule 9 to derive a CS block;

- Finally, rule 2.e is used to reduce those blocks that represent operations performed by the server before it starts processing requests. As a result the whole shaded subgraph of Figure 4.7-A is reduced to one single node (the block labeled c24) representing, at a higher level of abstraction, the client-server pattern (Figure 4.7-C).

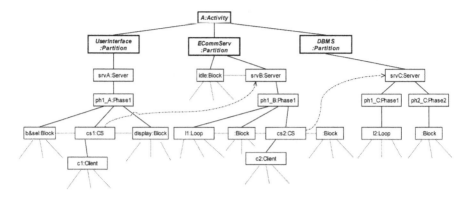

Figure 4.8. *The Abstract Syntax Tree constructed by parsing the source model*

At each reduction step, the performance annotations attached to the elements in the host graph are taken into account so that the information they contain is suitably propagated to the newly created elements and eventually to the nodes of the AST. For instance, when a sequence of blocks is reduced by rule 3, the demands of the two *rhs* blocks are added and the resulting demand value is associated with the new "sequence" non-terminal. Similarly, when applying rule 5, the number of repetitions is multiplied with the demand value of the cycle body block. The result is associated with the "loop" non-terminal from which a suitable node is created in the AST.

A simplified fragment of the AST is shown in Figure 4.8. A few notational conventions have been used so as so not to clutter the figure: the horizontal dotted lines that join nodes belonging to the same level, represent predecessor-successor associations (for those cases where such concept applies); also a curved dashed line breaks the tree structure and joins *CS* nodes (placed in the same subtree as their *Client*) with their *Server* part.

4.5.2. *Generating the LQN by relational mapping*

The outcome of the parsing phase is an extended model, which contains both the original elements from the UML source model and the elements from the AST generated by parsing. From a practical point of view, the extended model can be considered as a valid instance of the extended metamodel. This implies that, no matter what their nature is (i.e. whether they come from the original input model or not), the elements from the extended model can be used as a source for mapping. At the same time, the extended metamodel is defined in such a way that the original standard UML portion remains unmodified, and therefore compliant with the standard specification. Since the grammar rules and the construction of the AST are devised to analyze and extend the source in a way that is target-specific, the non-terminals identified (especially those included in the AST) are semantically closer to the target domain than the standard UML elements. This eases significantly the mapping from the extended source model to the target analysis domain. In fact, by parsing the source model the nodes *c2*, *ph1_c*, *ph2_c* and *cs2* are added to the AST (Figure 4.8), derived respectively from the non-terminals *b4, b9, b11, b14* (from Figure 4.7). They represent the client-server interaction between the e-commerce server and the DBMS, and more precisely the client behaviour (*c2*), the two phases of the server-side behaviour *(ph1_c* and *ph2_c)* and the CS interaction as a whole (*cs2*).

Two examples of QVT rules are presented in Figure 4.9. More rules have been omitted due to space constraints. The source patterns[1] are defined in terms of classes from the extended metamodel, and thus they can match any element in the extended source model, be it an AST element or any other instance of UML standard metaclasses. The rule execution order can be constrained by the conditions contained in the when/where clauses. For instance, the rule in Figure 4.9.a defines a relation between a client/server source element and an LQN RequestArc that joins the phase of the LQN entry representing the client that makes the request and the server entry that is requested. Such a relation is enforced only if the preconditions stated in the *when* clause are met.

The first precondition requires that a relation already exists between the model element stereotyped «PAresource» corresponding to the partition to which the CS element belongs, and the client task in the LQN model. A similar constraint mandates that a relation exists between the server side of the interaction and the task corresponding to the server in the target model. After the rule is successfully applied, the relations in the where clause are enforced in turn, mapping the client and the server elements in the source model to their respective entries in the target model. Figure 4.9.b shows another rule, which maps the first phase of a server's behaviour in the extended source model to the first phase of the entry representing the server in the LQN model. The when clause of the rule requires that a relationship already exists between the server to whom Phase 1 belongs and the LQN entry that owns the Phase element in the target model.

---

[1] We can use the terms *source/target* patterns without ambiguity, since the relation is *enforced* (E) only from the extended UML model to LQN, and just *checked* (C) in the opposite direction.

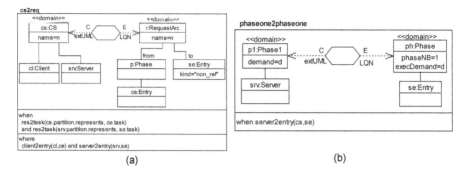

Figure 4.9. *QVT relation examples between the extended source model and the target model*

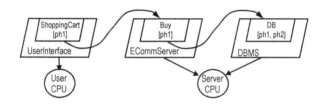

Figure 4.10. *LQN model for the case study system*

4.6. Conclusion

In this chapter we tackled the problem of abstraction-raising transformation for deriving analysis-oriented models from design specifications of software systems. The proposed approach addresses the need to bridge the significant semantic gap that usually exists between the domain of software design (source) and the domain of performance analysis (target). For this purpose, we introduced a method based on graph parsing that can significantly reduce the complexity of mappings from source to target models. This can be achieved using graph grammar rules to parse the source model and to extract from it additional elements that *explicitly* represent "abstractions" which are semantically closer to the target domain. As an example, we showed that our approach is successful in simplifying the definition of transformations from UML 2 models to LQNs, when a suitable graph grammar has been defined. Our proposal is amenable to seamless integration into standard MOF-based transformation frameworks, by making the parsing and the extension of the source model as a pre-processing step of a "conventional" model transformation pipeline. Another goal of the proposed abstraction-raising approach is to keep the original UML model intact; any extension of the source model with domain-specific concepts with the purpose to facilitate the transformation to the target model is recorded only in the Abstract Syntax Tree and does not affect the UML (meta)model. We are in the process of developing a prototype that implements the abstraction-raising transformation proposed in the paper.

Acknowledgments

This work was done during Antonino Sabetta's visit to Carleton University, Ottawa, with the financial support of NSERC Canada through its Discovery and Strategic Grant programs, of the MIUR-FIRB project "PERF: Performance evaluation of complex systems: techniques, methodologies and tools" and of the MIUR project "Model driven design and analysis of adaptable software architectures".

4.7. References

[BAL 04] Balsamo, S., Di Marco, A., Inverardi, P., Simeoni, M., "Model-based performance prediction in software development: a survey" IEEE Transactions on Software Engineering, Vol. 30, N.5, pp.295-310, May 2004.

[BER 02] S. Bernardi, S. Donatelli, and J. Merseguer, "From UML sequence diagrams and statecharts to analysable Petri net models" in Proc. 3rd Int. Workshop on Software and Performance (WOSP02), pp. 35-45, Rome, July 2002.

[CAV 04] C. Cavenet, S. Gilmore, J. Hillston, L. Kloul, and P. Stevens, "Analysing UML 2.0 activity diagrams in the software performance engineering process" in Proc. 4th Int. Workshop on Software and Performance (WOSP 2004), pp. 74-83, Redwood City, CA, Jan 2004.

[CZA 03] K. Czarnecki and S. Helsen, "Classification of Model Transformation Approaches", OOPSLA'03 Workshop on Generative Techniques in the Context of Model-Driven Architecture, 2003.

[GRA 05] V. Grassi, R. Mirandola, A.Sabetta, "From Design to Analysis Models: A Kernel Language for Performance and Reliability Analysis of Component-based Systems", In Proc. 5th Int. Workshop on Software and Performance WOSP'2005, pp. 25-36, Palma, Spain, July 2005.

[JUR 04] J. Jürjens, P. Shabalin, "Automated Verification of UMLsec Models for Security Requirements", Proceedings of UML 2004, Lisbon, Portugal, Oct. 11–15, 2004.

[KUS 04] J.M. Kuster, S. Sendall, M. Wahler, "Comparing Two Model Transformation Approaches", Proc. Workshop on OCL and Model Driven Engineering, October, 2004.

[MEN 05] T. Mens, K. Czarnecki, P. Van Gorp, "A Taxonomy of Model transformations", in Proc. of Dagstuhl 04101 Language Engineering for Model-Driven Software Development (J. Bezivin, R. Heckel eds.), 2005.

[OMG 03] Object Management Group, "MDA Guide", version 1.0.1, June 2003.

[OMG 05a] Object Management Group, "UML Profile for Schedulability, Performance, and Time", version 1.1, OMG document formal/05-01-02, January 2005.

[OMG 05b] Object Management Group, "MOF QVT – Final Adopted Specification", OMG document ptc/2005-11-01, November 2005.

[OMG 05c] Object Management Group, "RFP for UML Profile for Modeling and Analysis of Real-Time and Embedded systems (MARTE)", realtime/05-02-06, December 2005.

[PET 02] D.C. Petriu, H.Shen, "Applying the UML Performance Profile: Graph Grammar based derivation of LQN models from UML specifications", in Computer Performance Evaluation (T. Fields, P. Harrison, J. Bradley, U. Harder, Eds.) LNCS 2324, pp.159-177, Springer, 2002.

[PET 03] D. C. Petriu, C. M. Woodside, "Performance Analysis with UML", in UML for Real, (B. Selic, L. Lavagno, and G. Martin, eds.), pp. 221-240, Kluwer, 2003.

[REK 97] J. Rekers, A. Schürr, "Defining and Parsing Visual Languages with Layered Graph Grammars", Journal of Visual Languages & Computing, Vol. 8, No 1, pp. 27-55(29), Academic Press, 1997.

[ROL 95] Rolia, J.A., Sevcik, K.C., The Method of Layers, IEEE Trans. on Software Eng., Vol. 21, Nb. 8, pp. 689-700, 1995.

[ROZ 97] G. Rozenberg, "Handbook of graph grammars and computing by graph transformation: volume I. foundations", World Scientific Publishing Co., 1997.

[SAB 05] A. Sabetta, D.C. Petriu, V. Grassi and R. Mirandola "Abstraction-raising Transformation for Generating Analysis Models", in Proc. of MoDELS 2005 Satellite Events, Lecture Notes in Computer Science, Springer, 2005.

[WOO 95] Woodside, C.M., Neilson, J.E., Petriu, D.C., Majumdar, S., "The Stochastic Rendezvous Network Model for Performance of Synchronous Client-Server-like Distributed Software", IEEE Trans. on Computers, Vol.44, Nb.1, pp. 20-34, 1995.

[WOO 05] Woodside, C.M, Petriu, D.C., Petriu, D.B., Shen, H, Israr, T., and Merseguer, J., "Performance by Unified Model Analysis (PUMA)", in Proc. 5th Int. Workshop on Software and Performance WOSP'2005, pp.1-12, Palma, Spain, July 2005.

CHAPTER 5

Component-Based Software Engineering for Embedded Systems

Chapter written by Ivica Crnkovic

Department of Computer Science and Electronics
Mälardalen University, Box 883, Västerås, Sweden,
http://www.idt.mdh.se/~icc
ivica.crnkovic@mdh.se

5.1. Embedded systems

Embedded systems cover a large range of computer systems from ultra small computer-based devices to large systems monitoring and controlling complex processes. The overwhelming number of computer systems belongs to embedded systems: 98% of all computer systems belong to embedded systems today. This is not a surprise; when we look around us we found a number of devices, instruments, machines that contain built in computers: mobile telephones, TV-sets and all other entertainment devices, cars, cash dispensers, microwave owns, washing machines, watches, etc. In addition to such devices we have large systems such as traffic control systems, power station systems, airplanes, telecommunication systems, energy distribution systems, etc. All these systems belong to a category of embedded systems. What are embedded systems then? We can use a definition from IEEE:

An Embedded Computer System: A computer system that is part of a larger system and performs some of the requirements of that system; for example, a computer system used in an aircraft or rapid transit system, (IEEE, 1992).

Most of such embedded systems can also be characterized as real-time systems, (i.e., systems in which the correctness of the system depends not only on the logical result of the computations it performs but also on time factors [STA 98]). Embedded real-time systems contain a computer as a part of a larger system and interact directly with external devices. They must usually meet stringent specifications for safety, reliability, limited hardware capacity, low development and production costs, etc. The increased complexity of embedded real-time systems leads to increasing demands with respect to requirements engineering, high-level design, early error detection, productivity, integration, verification and maintenance.

Component-based development is an attractive approach in the domains of embedded systems. As for other domains there are two main benefits specific to component technology. First, it gives structure to system design and system development, thus making system verification and maintenance more efficient. Second, it allows reuse of development effort by allowing components to be reused across products and in the longer term it enables building a market for software components. In particular for the development of many variants of products the component-based approach is attractive. In spite of this attractiveness the adoption of component-based technologies for the development of real-time and embedded systems is significantly slower. Major reasons are that embedded systems must satisfy requirements of timeliness, quality-of-service, predictability, that they are often safety-critical, and can use severely constrained resources (memory, processing power, communication). The widely used component technologies such as EJB, .NET, CORBA component models are inherently heavyweight and complex, incurring large overheads on the run-time platform; they do not in general address timeliness, quality-of-service or similar extra-functional properties that are important for real-time systems. In their present form they start to be deployed in large, distributed, and not safety critical systems, e.g., in industrial automation, but are not suitable for deployment in most embedded real-time environments.

5.2. Specific requirement and aspects of Embedded Systems

In most of the cases embedded systems are real-time systems. In many cases embedded systems are safety or mission critical systems. Embedded systems vary from very small systems to very large systems. For small systems there are strong constrains related to different recourses such as power or memory consumption. For these as well as for large embedded systems the demands on reliability, robustness, availability and other characteristics of dependable systems are important. Finally, in many domains, the product life cycle is very long – in can stretch to several decades.

All these characteristics have strong implications on requirements. Most of the requirements of embedded systems are related to non-functional characteristics (better designated as extra-functional properties). These properties can be classified in run-time and life cycle extra-functional properties. Let us look at some of these properties:

- *Real-time properties*: The real-time system functions are time-related; a violation of time requirements even of a proper functional response violates the functionality of the system. There are numbers of real-time properties: response time or latency identifies the time needed for a function to provide an output triggered by an input. Execution time defines the time of an execution of a function. A worst case execution time is the guaranteed time within the function will be executed. A deadline is the time point at which a function, if not already completed, is being interrupted or stopped. These properties are used to express the behavior of the system and for verification that real-time requirements are met.

- *Dependability*: Dependability is defined as an ability of a system to deliver service that can justifiably be trusted and an ability of a system to avoid failures that are more severe and frequent than is acceptable to the users. The main means to attain dependability are related to avoidance of faults: fault prevention, fault tolerance, fault removal and fault forecasting [AVI 01]. Dependability is characterised by several attributes and according to [AVI 01], these are the following: reliability, availability, integrity, safety, confidentiality and maintainability. All these attributes are run-time properties except maintainability. Reliability is specified as a probability that a system fails in a given period of time. The reliability is reverse proportional to this probability as mean time to failure and it is defined for a specified period of time under stated conditions. Availability is defined as the probability of a system being available when needed. Formally it is defined as a mean time to failure divided by mean time between failures, which in turn is a sum of mean time to failure and mean time to repair. Safety is the property in which the interaction with the environment and possible consequences of the system failure are considered. Confidentiality is defined as absence of unauthorized disclosure of information and integrity as an absence of improper system alternations. From their definitions we can see that these attributes are combination of several properties. For example, availability is dependent on real-time properties, but also on reliability and even maintenance; safety is strongly related to reliability, etc. This introduces difficulties in specification of requirements as well as in measurements and specification of the properties themselves.

- *Resource consumption*: Many embedded systems have strong requirements for low and controlled consumption of different resources. The reasons may be the size of the systems and/or the demands on lower production costs. In many domains these requirements have a decisive impact on the design of these systems and even on the programming techniques. Examples of such restrictions and constraints are power and memory consumption, execution (CPU) time, computation (CPU) power, etc.

- *Life cycle properties*: In general embedded systems are tightly coupled with their environment and the absence of their services can have large consequences on the environment. In many domains the embedded systems have very long lifetime running round the clock year after year. These characteristics have a strong impact on requirements, design and implementation of these systems. For example, maintainability and modifiability are essential for a large range of embedded systems. During the lifetime of a system several generations of hardware and software technologies can be used. The long life systems must be able to cope with these changes introduced either into the surrounding environment or into the systems themselves.

We can conclude that many requirements of the embedded systems are related to extra-functional properties. This has an implication that development and maintenance of such systems are very costly. In particular activities related to verification and guaranteed behaviour (formal verification, modelling, tests, etc.) and maintenance (adaptive maintenance, debugging, regressive testing, etc.) require a lot of efforts. For these reasons the technologies and processes that lead to lower costs for these activities are very attractive and desirable.

5.3. Component-based Basic Concepts for Embedded Systems

A basic idea in component based software development is to structure a system into components. In classic engineering disciplines, a component is a self-contained part or subsystem that can be used as a building block in the design of a larger system. It provides specified services to its environment across well-specified interfaces. Ideally, the development of components should be decoupled from the development of the systems that contain them. Components should be reusable in different contexts.

In software engineering, there are many different suggestions for precise definitions of components in component based software development. According to [BAC 00], advocates of software reuse equate components to anything that can be reused; practitioners using commercial off-the shelf (COTS) software equate components to COTS products; software methodologists equate components with units of project and configuration management; and software architects equate components with design abstractions.

The best accepted definition in the software industry world is based on Szyperski's work [SZY 98]:

A component is a unit of composition with contractually specified interfaces and fully explicit context dependencies that can be deployed independently and is subject to third-party composition.

Szyperski tends to emphasize that components should be delivered in binary form, and that deployment and composition should be performed at run-time. However, in the second edition of his book [SZY 02], Szyperski extends the binary form to a more general "executable".

In the domains of embedded systems this definition is largely followed, in particular the separation between component implementation and component interface. However, the demands on the binary or executable form are not directly followed. A component can be delivered in a form of a source code written in a high-level language, and allows build-time (or design-time) composition. This more liberal view is partly motivated by the embedded systems context, as will be discussed below.

Many important properties of components in embedded systems, such as timing and performance, depend on characteristics of the underlying hardware platform. Kopetz and Suri [KOP 03] propose to distinguish between software components and system components. Extra-functional properties, such as performance, cannot be specified for a software component in isolation. Such properties must either be specified with respect to a given hardware platform, or be parameterized on (characteristics of) the underlying platform. A system component is defined as a self-contained hardware and software subsystem, and can satisfy both functional and extra-functional properties.

5.4. Specific Demands on Component-based Software Engineering

The specific characteristics of embedded systems lead to specific requirements of component technologies. In particular the approaches in development process and component specifications using interfaces are different from those implemented in the component technologies widely used in other domains.

5.4.1. *Component Interface*

Ideally a component interface specifies all properties of a component that are externally visible to the other parts of the system. An interface may list the signatures of operations, in which case it can be used to check that components interact without causing type mismatches. An interface may contain additional information about the component's patterns of interaction with its environment or about extra-functional properties such as execution time; this allows more system properties to be determined when the system is first designed. An interface that, in addition to information about operation signatures, also specifies behavioural or extra-functional properties is called a rich interface.

The information in component interfaces facilitates the check for interoperability between components. Rich interfaces enable verification of system requirements and prediction of system properties from properties of components. This allows several system properties to be verified and predicted early in the development life cycle, enables early design space exploration, and saves significant effort in the later system integration phase.

5.4.2. *Component deployment and composition*

In widely used component technologies, the interfaces are usually implemented as object interfaces supporting polymorphism by late binding. While late binding enables connecting of components that are completely unaware of each other beside the connecting interface, this flexibility comes with a performance penalty which may be difficult to carry for small embedded systems. Therefore the dynamic component deployment is not feasible for small embedded systems.

Taking into account all the constraints for real-time and embedded systems, we conclude that there are several reasons to perform component deployment and composition at design time rather than run-time [CRN 02]:

- This allows composition tools to generate a monolithic firmware for the device from the component-based design;

- This allows for global optimizations: e.g., in a static component composition known at design time, connections between components could be translated into direct function calls instead of using dynamic event notifications;

- Design-time composition could be the instance of specific adaptation of components and generated code towards specific micro controller families and real-time operating systems APIs;

- Verification and prediction of system requirements can be done statically from the given component properties;

- Design time composition presupposes a composition environment that specifically provides the following functionalities;

- Component composition support;

- Component adaptation and code generation for the application;

- Building the system by including selected components and components that are part of the run-time framework;

- Static verification and prediction of system requirements and properties from the given component properties.

There may also be a need for a run-time environment, which supports the component framework by a set of services. The framework enables component intercommunication (those aspects which are not performed at design time), and (where relevant) control of the behaviour of the components.

Figure 5.1 shows different environments in a component life cycle. The figure is adopted from [CRN 02].

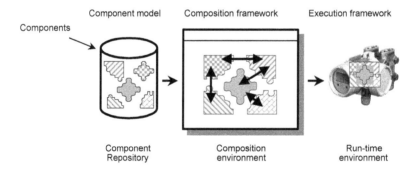

Figure 5.1. *Component technology for embedded systems*

5.5. State of the CBSE practice and experience for Embedded Systems

Types of embedded systems vary from ultra small devices with simple functionality, through small systems with sophisticated functions, to large, possibly distributed systems, where the management of the complexity is the main challenge. Further we can distinguish between systems produced in large quantities, in which the low production costs are very important and low-volume products in which the system dependability is the most important feature. All these different requirements have impact on feasibility, on use, and on approach in component-based development. In different domains we can find very different component models and system and software architectures. This chapter gives some examples of use of CBSE in several industry domains.

5.5.1. *Automotive Industry*

The automotive domains constitute a branch of vehicular systems, were vehicular systems are the systems that are mobile and that carry engines that provide this mobility. Example of vehicular systems domains are avionics, automotive industry, train industry and even mobile robots. Embedded systems in these domains have many similarities in principles, but also many differences which are the results of their respective business nature. For example, in the automotive industry the main requirement is low product cost, while safety is the most important requirement in avionics. The similarities between these domains are the type of embedded systems used- it is about controllers – systems that monitor and control a particular process.

Embedded control systems have grown from stand-alone controllers to distributed control systems. The growth has been "bottom-up" in nature. The result is that of a sudden increase in both possibilities and interaction problems. At the same time the costs for development of electronics of which the vast part is software development increases dramatically, and today it is reaching about 40% of total costs with a tendency for further increase [GRI 03]. An example of software costs vs. total development cost for the Mercedes-Benz family is shown on Figure 5.2.

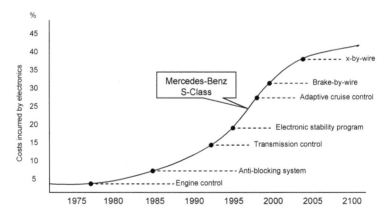

Figure 5.2. *Proportion of costs incurred by electronics [GRI 03]*

Within the automotive industry, the component-based approach has a relatively long tradition, as these systems are typically built from system components that are either developed in-house or provided by external suppliers. Today, the entire control system of an advanced car includes a number of ECUs equipped with software that implements vehicle functions (see Figure 5.3). ECUs are treated as system components that can be developed and build independently of each other and of the entire system.

As the number of ECUs increases, the entire system becomes more complex. In addition, new advanced functions (for example a cruise control) require input and output control from many ECUs. This requires sharing different types of resources (sensors, actuators, time, communication, memory, and CPU consumption). With increasing complexity, maintaining the system reliability and safety become major problems. A satisfactory handling of safety-critical functions, such as emerging brake and steer-by-wire systems, will require the integration of methods for establishing components and compositions of different aspects: functional and temporal correctness, safety and reliability, etc.

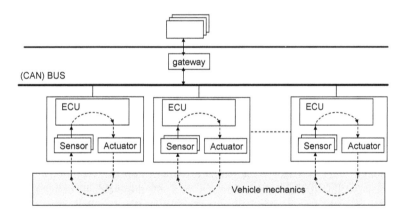

Figure 5.3. *Component-based architecture of vehicular systems*

Even if the component-based approach is strong on the system level, this is not true for software development. ECUs include proprietary software, mostly owned by subcontractors. This makes the entire system inflexible and inefficient in utilizing resources, makes it difficult to implement complex functions, and expensive to add new ECUs. The next major step in designing these systems is to go from the current situation with one node, one supplier to a situation with one node, several suppliers. Furthermore, to enable delivery of more complex applications, it should be possible to spread out software components through several nodes. This requires changes in the design process and a new division of responsibilities. For example, development of software components should be separated form development of hardware components (ECUs). To obtain this a component model and an infrastructure (middleware) should be standardized. Developing and establishing an appropriate component technology, including a supporting framework, is one of the main research challenges.

The ECU is the most obvious and common notion of a component in vehicular electronic systems. The software components are, in this view, the binaries for the ECUs. Since the ECU is the unit of integration each supplier of an ECU can develop the internal behaviour using any technology, such as Simulink, plain C-code, RTOS and C-code, etc. Therefore, there have been no incitements for creating a standard for ECU software development.

Vehicles present a heterogeneous environment where the interaction between the computer system and the vehicle take different forms. Some vehicle functionality requires periodic execution of software, e.g., feedback control, whereas other functionality has a sporadic nature, e.g., alarms. Although vehicle control plays a central role, there is also an abundance of other functionality in vehicles that is less critical and has other characteristics, e.g., requires more flexibility. Although less critical, many of these functions will still interact with other more critical parts of the control system; consider for example diagnostics.

Given this background, the lack of a standardised software component technology for vehicle electronic systems come as no surprise. Currently there are ongoing industrial and research projects in defining component models and system architectures (AUTOSAR, www.autosar.org/, or SAVE [AKE 06]).

Although there is a lack of a standardised and holistic technology, there exist component technologies specialising on part of the vehicle functionality. For continuous control a computational model based on the data flow style is common and results in simple application descriptions and system implementations that are relatively straightforward to analyse and verify. The data flow style is commonly used within the embedded systems domain, e.g., in IEC 61131 used for automation [IEC 95] and in Simulink used for control modelling. Current research presents several component technologies for embedded systems in general but also dedicated technologies for vehicular systems, but there are few commercially available technologies.

One example of commercially available technologies that are used within the vehicle industry is the Rubus component technology [CRN 02]. A basic Rubus software component can be used as units of independent reuse and consists of a set of in-ports and out-ports, an entry function defining the behaviour, and a persistent state. The thread of execution for a component is provided by a Rubus task. The component interface in the Rubus component model is port based. Components communicate with each others through typed data ports, and on activation a component reads the data on its in-port, executes its function and finally writes the result of the computation to its out-port. In Rubus there are also non-functional interfaces, with which timing properties are defined. The non-functional interfaces specify release-time, deadline, worst case execution times and a period time. During system design it is also possible to define precedence relations, ordering and mutual exclusion.

5.5.2. *Industrial Automation*

In the last five years the use of component-based technologies has rapidly expanded and become the dominating development technologies in industrial automation. The technology mostly used in large systems is Microsoft COM and recently .NET, and to smaller extent different implementations of CORBA, although no one of these technologies provide support for real-time. The systems using these technologies belong to the category of soft-real time systems. Often a component technology is used as a basis for additional abstraction level support, which is specified either as standards or proprietary solutions. For hard and small real-time systems the component-based approach is still in its rudimentary phase.

The main reason for wide use of component-based technology in the automation industry is the possibility of reusing solutions in different ranges of products, efficient development tools, standardized specifications and interoperation, and integration between different products.

One successful example of adoption of a component-based technology is the initiative OPC Foundation (OLE process control Foundation, www.opcfoundation.org), an organization that consists of more than 300 member companies worldwide, is responsible for a specification that defines a set of standard interfaces based upon Microsoft's OLE/COM and recently .NET technology. OPC consists of a standard set of interfaces, properties, and methods for use in process-control and manufacturing-automation applications. OPC provides a common interface for communicating with diverse process-control devices, regardless of the controlling software or devices in the process. The application of the OPC standard interface enables interoperability between automation/control applications, field systems/devices and business/office applications. OPC addresses the problem of integration of different small devices and control systems in large control systems. A key reason for this problem is that interfaces are not standard. Proprietary systems that do not communicate among each other are fairly common. Hardware and software choices for process and industrial manufacturers are sharply reduced because their application suppliers provide limited connectivity. As a solution to this problem OPC proposes a standard that provides plug-and-play software technology for process control and factory automation where every system, every device and every driver can freely connect and communicate. However, this flexibility can introduce more uncertainty in the system, so for dependable and hard-real time system this technology must be used very carefully. The basic principle is simple. The providers of the control devices also deliver services that comply with OPC standards. Applications use standard OPC interfaces and there is no need to write drives or adapter to them in the application. The same interfaces can be used for a range of devices. In addition, application can easily use (and replace) devices from different vendors as the same standardized interfaces are used.

Another example of a component-based approach is the development and use of the standard IEC 61131 [IEC 95] successfully used in development of industrial process automation systems, for example in ABB, Siemens Bombardier Transportation, etc.

Process automation systems that must fulfill real-time requirements usually do not use component-based technologies. However, in some cases, such as for ABB controllers, a reduced version of COM has been used on a top of a real-time operating system [LUD 02]. The reduced version includes facilities for component specification using the interface description language (IDL), and some basic services at run-time such as component deployment has been used. These services have been implemented internally. Different communication protocols and I/O drivers have been identified as components.

5.5.3. *Consumer Electronics*

Consumer electronics products, such as TV, VCR, and DVD, are developed and delivered in form of product families which are characterized by many similarities and few differences and in form of product populations which are sets of products with many similarities but also many differences. Production is organized into product lines – this allows many variations on a central product definition. A product line is a top-down, planned, proactive approach to achieve reuse of software within a family or population of products. It is based on use of a common architecture and core functions included into the product platform and basic components. The diversity of products is achieved by inclusion of different components. Because of the requirements for low hardware and production costs, general-purpose component technologies have not been used, but rather more dedicated and simpler propriety models have been developed. There are two main benefits in a product line development: (i) reuse of already existing components and common architecture; (ii) separation of product development from component development. The first benefit is achieved not only through reuse of the core functionality (which includes the architecture solutions and components that build a core-functionality), but also reuse of particular components in different product families. The second benefit is realized by enabling larger development time for particular components than the time for development of a specific product.

An example of such a component model is the Koala component model used at Philips [OMM 00, OMM 02]. Koala is a component model and an architectural description language to build a large diversity of products from a repository of components. Koala is designed to build consumer products such as televisions, video recorders, CD and DVD players and recorders, and combinations of them. A Koala component is a piece of code that can interact with its environment through explicit interfaces only. The implementation of a Koala component is a directory with a set of C and header files that may use each other in arbitrary ways, but communication with other components is achieved only through header files generated by the Koala compiler, based upon the binding between components. As Koala components are delivered in source code, it is possible to statically analyze components and systems built of them. Figure 5.4 shows a graphical presentation of a Koala component (CC) composed of several basic components (C1, C2, C3). We can recognise component interfaces (provided and required) and glue code (denoted as m and s).

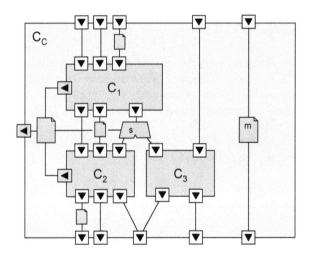

Figure 5.4. *Example of a Koala component [CRN 02]*

The component models used in consumer electronics are proprietary, which requires internal support for their development and maintenance. Further it requires development of a number of development tools: component repository, composition languages, compilers, debugging and testing tools, configuration tools, etc. Such development is usually not a core business and it requires a lot of resources. In addition, the use of a proprietary technology makes it more difficult to use COTS components. There are increasing requirements for achieving interoperability between proprietary and standard component technologies. The component models used in consumer electronics support only rudimentary analysis and prediction of extra-functional properties of the components and systems.

5.5.4. Other domains

There are many domains in which embedded systems are used extensively. Some of them are: telecommunications, avionics and aerospace, transportation, computer games, home electronics, navigation systems, etc. While there are many similarities between these domains, there are also very different requirements for their functional and extra-functional properties. The consequences are that the requirements for component-based technologies are different, and consequently we cannot expect to have one component model. The expectations are that many component models will coexist, sharing to greater or lesser extents some common characteristics, such as basic principles of component specifications through interfaces, basic composition and run-time services, certain patterns, and similar features.

5.6. Work on standardization

Standardization (and research) work for component-based approach in embedded systems can be classified in three categories: work on general standards which are adopted by CBSE communities, work on standards for embedded systems that are applicable for CBSE and to a smaller extent work on standardization of CBSE for embedded systems.

5.6.1. The Unified Modelling Language (UML)

The Unified Modelling Language (UML) is the de-facto industry language for specifying and designing software systems. UML now provides support for a wide variety of modelling domains, including real-time system modelling and is used more and more in different domains of embedded systems.

Currently a work on standardisation of UML 2.0 is ongoing within OMG (www.omg.org). The aim is that UML should become a family of languages, each based on a common semantic core, i.e. specific variants of UML will be defined for specific application areas: e-business, real-time, systems engineering, etc. Another important aim is that UML 2.0 should be defined more precisely in order to facilitate the more rigorous use of the language. The standardization addresses the following main areas: infrastructure (the core modeling concepts supported by UML), superstructure (the modeling concepts that are used to model specific views of a system, e.g., state behavior), OCL (the object constraint language that supports the semi-formal specification of constraints) and diagram interchange (tool interchange of diagrammatical syntax).

Components in UML 2.0 will get a more extensive treatment than in previous versions of UML. A component will be defined as a superstructure on a meta level. UML 2.0 components will become a modular part of a system that may be modelled and refined throughout the development life cycle. A component is identified as an autonomous unit within a system or subsystem. It has one or more ports, and its internals are hidden and inaccessible other than as provided by its interfaces. The interfaces are divided into required and provided interfaces. As a result the components can be flexibly reused and replaced. Components also support reuse through an import mechanism, which allows the elements of a component to be imported into another component. UML 2.0 component model comprises characteristics of component models which thus makes it possible to use UML as modelling language or ADL to support CBSE design methodology.

Real-time aspects are another focus in UML 2.0. OMG has initiated a work to define a UML profile specific to real-time systems development. The real-time UML profile [OMG 01] (actually the profile for Schedulability, Performance, and Time Specification) defines standard paradigms of use for modelling of time-, schedulability-, and performance-related aspects of real-time systems. The intention is to: (i) enable the construction of models that could be used to make quantitative predictions regarding these characteristics, (ii) facilitate communication of design intent between developers in a standard way, and (iii) enable interoperability between various analysis and design tools. However, UML 2.0 does not provide direct support for modelling extra-functional properties.

It can be worthwhile mentioning that the real-time UML profile does not use components as a basic structure and it remains open as to how to map components and their properties to real-time properties.

The Model Driven Architecture (MDA) is the OMG's new architecture that aims to integrate its standards within a model driven approach to system development [SIE 01]. MDA encapsulates many important ideas – most notably the notion that real benefits can be obtained by using modelling languages to integrate the huge diversity of languages used in the development of systems. In MDA, modelling languages are categorized as being platform independent, i.e. specification oriented. Examples of platform independent languages include UML itself (when used for specification). Middleware standards such as CORBA and programming level languages (e.g. Java Beans) are examples of platform specific languages. Even if it is not well defined today, it seems that components will also play a role in structuring MDA basic parts (documents, profiles and tools). We can expect identification of "MDA-Components" whose nature could be clarified thanks standard stereotypes such as Tool, UML Profile and Document.

5.6.2. *Real-time CORBA*

Real-time CORBA is an extension to CORBA that is designed for applications with real-time requirements. Real-time CORBA has a particular benefit to the embedded, real-time systems market, as until recently, many such systems have had to define highly platform specific approaches to implementing many of the features proposed by the CORBA standard. Since CORBA includes CORBA Component Model specification, Real-time CORBA can be combined with it encouraging component-based approach in real-time applications. Real-time CORBA provides standard interfaces and policies that allow applications to configure and control the following system resources:

(i)   Processor resources via thread pools, priority mechanisms, intra-process mutexes, and a global scheduling service for real-time applications with fixed priorities;

(ii)   Communication resources via protocol properties and explicit bindings to server objects using priority bands and private connections;

(iii)   Memory resources via buffering requests in queues and bounding the size of thread pools CORBA and real-time.

Real-time CORBA is in itself only a standard for controlling system resources. It is up to the system designer to use the standard to configure the system to meet application requirements in a predictable way. Real-time CORBA has some limitations such as not being suitable for dynamic real-time systems since it is only focused on fixed-priority based systems, and such as not addressing consistency issues. RT-CORBA only addresses static distributed systems whose resource requirements are known a priori. OMGs Dynamic Scheduling proposal [OMG 01] intends is to overcome the limitations imposed by Real-time CORBA in terms of dynamic scheduling.

5.6.3. *Programmable Logic Controllers: the IEC 61131-3 standard*

In the area of Industrial Automation, PLCs (Programmable Logic Controllers) are a widely used technology. IEC 61131 has received worldwide international and industrial acceptance for programming these types, but also more sophisticated types of controllers. Certified IEC 61131-3 programming systems have an agreed degree of source code compatibility and have a similar look and feel. An international organization of users and producers, PLCopen (www.plcopen.org), founded in 1992 offers tests for IEC 61131-3 compliance.

IEC 61131 comprises a set of languages. There are two textual languages (Structured Text, Instruction List) and three graphical languages (Function Block Diagram, Ladder Diagram, Sequential Function). A basic entity in these languages is a functional block. A functional block can be seen as a component. Each functional block has a set of in-ports and out-ports. IEC 61131-3 also requires strong data typing and provides support to define data structures, which can be used to transmit information as a whole between different units. Function block execution may be periodic or event-driven. There is no support for analyzing other properties than syntactic properties.

The IEC 61131-3 standard is widely used. Compared with traditional programming systems, it appears to be a major step forward. However, the IEC 61131-3 standard is not fully mature and the portability issue is still an important problem. Furthermore, some ambiguous semantics remain for the languages. Also, new requirements emerge: systems will become more distributed with more parallel processing. New standards are under development, such as the function block standard IEC 1499, not to replace the former but to work in conjunction with it.

5.6.4. *Other standards and de-facto standards*

There are many standards and de-facto standards in the component-based, middleware, software architecture, etc. domains that are not specific for embedded systems, but are considered in embedded systems areas. Some of them are EDOC (a UML Profile for Enterprise Distributed Object Computing [OMG1 01]), XML, SOAP, TAO CORBA and EJB [WAN 00]. In contrast to other domains, embedded systems often address both hardware (system) and software level by the same design tools or language in the development process. Examples of such tools are MetaH (www.htc.honeywell.com/metah) which is a domain-specific ADL dedicated to avionics systems, SystemC (www.systemc.org) which is intended to be a standardized, highly portable technology for system-level models, VHDL, a hardware description language, etc.

5.7. The needs and priorities in research

Major needs for the further development of component technology for embedded systems are the following [BOU 05]:

- Need for adopted component models and frameworks for embedded systems. A problem is that many application domains have application-dependent requirements on such a technology;

- Need for light-weight implementations of component frameworks. In order to support more advanced features in component-based systems, the run-time platform must provide certain services, which however must use only limited resources;

- Uniform Specification of Rich Interfaces: current specification techniques for contracts use notations and models that are quite different. It is very desirable to achieve unification and uniformization of such notations;

- Obtaining extra-functional properties of components: timing and performance properties are usually obtained from components by measurement, usually by means of simulation. Problems with this approach are that the results depend crucially on the environment (model) used for the measurements may not be valid in other environments, and that the results may depend on factors which cannot easily be controlled. Techniques should be developed for overcoming these problems, thereby obtaining more reliable specifications of component properties;

- Platform and vendor independence: many current component technologies are rather tightly bound to a particular platform (either run-time platform or design platform). This means that components only make sense in the context of a particular platform;

- Efforts to predict system properties: the analysis of many global properties from component properties is hindered by inherent complexity issues. Efforts should be directed to finding techniques for coping with this complexity;

- Component certification: in order to transfer components across organizations, techniques and procedures should be developed for ensuring the trustworthiness of components;

- Component noninterference: particularly in safety-critical applications, there is a need to ensure separation and protection between component implementations, in terms of memory protection, resource usage, etc;

- Tool support: the adoption of component technology depends on the development of tool support.

The clearly identified priorities of CBSE for embedded systems are:

-   Predicting system properties. A research challenge today is to predict system properties from the component properties. This is interesting for system integration, to achieve predictability, etc;

-   Development of widely adopted component models for real-time systems. Such a model should be supported by technology for generating necessary runtime infrastructure (which must be light-weight), generation of monitors to check conformance with contracts, etc. The trend towards open an integrated systems implies that it should be possible for a system to use both a component model specific for real-time systems, and some of the widely used component technologies.

5.8. References

[AKE 06] Åkerholm M, et al., The SAVE approach to component-based development of vehicular systems, Journal of Systems and Software, Elsevier, May, 2006.

[AVI 01] Avižienis, A., Laprie, J-C., Randell, B., Fundamental Concepts of Computer System Dependability, IARP/IEEE-RAS Workshop on Robot Dependability: Technological Challenge of Dependable, Robots in Human Environments, 2001.

[BAC 00] Bachmann F., L. Bass, C. Buhman, S. Comella-Dorda, F. Long, J. Robert, R. Seacord, and K. Wallnau. Technical Concepts of Component-Based Software Engineering, Volume II. Technical Report CMU/SEI-2000-TR-008, Software Engineering Institute, Carnegie-Mellon University, May 2000.

[BOU 05] Bruno Bouyssounouse, Joseph Sifakis, Component-Based System Development - Embedded Systems Design, The ARTIST Roadmap for Research and Development, Volume 3436, Springer, ISBN: 3-540-25107-3, 2005.

[CRN 02] Crnkovic and M. Larsson. Building Reliable Component-Based Software Systems. ArtechHouse, 2002.

[GRI 03] Grimm K, Software technology in an automotive company: major challenges, Proceedings of the 25th international conference on Software engineering, 2003.

[IEC 95] IEC. Application and implementation of IEC 61131-3. Technical report, IEC, Geneva, 1995.

[KOP 03] H. Kopetz and N. Suri. Compositional design of RT systems: A conceptual basis for specification of linking interfaces. In Proc. 6th IEEE International Symposium on Object-oriented Real-Time Distributed Computing (ISORC), Hokkaido, Japan, May 2003.

[LUD 02] F. Lüders, I. Crnkovic, and A. Sjögren. Case study: Componentization of an industrial control system. In Proc. 26th Annual International Computer

Software and Applications Conference - COMPSAC 2002, Oxford, UK, IEEE Computer Society Press, Aug. 2002.

[OMG 01] OMG. Response to the OMG RFP for schedulability, performance, and time (revised submission). OMG, RFP ad/2001-06-14, June 2001.

[OMG1 01] OMG. A uml profile for enterprise distributed object computing. ptc/2001-12-04, June 18 2001.

[OMM 00] R. van Ommering, F. van der Linden, and J. Kramer. The Koala component model for consumer electronics software. IEEE Computer, 33(3):78–85, March 2000.

[OMM 02] R. van Ommering. Building product populations with software components. In Proceedings of the 24th international conference on Software engineering, ACM Press, 2002.

[SIE 01] Siegel J. and the O.S.S. Group. Developing in OMG's model-driven architecture. OMG, White paper, Revision 2.6, Nov. 2001.

[STA 98] Stankovic J. and Ramamritham K., "Tutorial on Hard Real-Time Systems", IEEE Computer Society Press, 1998.

[SZY 98] C. Szyperski. Component Software: Beyond Object-Oriented Programming. ACM, Press and Addison-Wesley, New York, N.Y., 1998.

[SZY 02] C. Szyperski. Component Software: Beyond Object-Oriented Programming. Second edition, ACM, Press and Addison-Wesley, New York, N.Y., 2002.

[WAN 00] N. Wang, D. Schmidt, and C. O'Ryan. Overview of the CORBA Component Model. White paper, Sept. 2000.

CHAPTER 6

Model Driven Engineering for System-on-Chip Design

Chapter written by Pierre Boulet, Cédric Dumoulin and Antoine Honoré

Laboratoire d'Informatique Fondamentale de Lille
USTL/CNRS/INRIA Futurs
Cité Scientifique
59655 Villeneuve d'Ascq cedex
http://www.lifl.fr/west/
{Pierre.Boulet,Cedric.Dumoulin,Antoine.Honore}@lifl.fr

6.1. Introduction

With the evolution of the manufacturing technologies, the semiconductor industry is able to build chips with several billions of transistors. Such very complex chips often integrate multiple cores (processing units, hardware accelerating functions, etc), memory (DRAM, flash, etc) and even non-digital design parts such as analog or radio frequency circuits or mechanical, chemical or biological devices (Micro/Nano Electro Mechanical Systems). These chips are called Systems-on-Chip (SoCs).

For the last few years, the semiconductor industry has faced a new problem: the design gap. Indeed, the time-to-market constraints are so tight that the design teams are not able to meaningfully use all the available transistors on a chip (at least for something else than highly regular structures as memory). For the consumer electronics, the typical time-to-market constraint is 6 to 12 months from the publication of a standard to the first implementation. With the ever increasing density of integration, this problem is getting worse and worse. Some significant increase in the designer's productivity is much needed.

We will first look more closely at the problems faced by SoC designers and why model driven engineering can help them in section 6.2. Then we will present the standardization efforts towards the definition of UML profiles that could help SoC designers in section 6.3. Section 6.4 will present a model driven based environment dedicated to SoC co-modeling for computation intensive applications partially based on some of these profiles and in section 6.5 we will outline the architecture of the software framework supporting this environment and the supporting tools.

6.2. SoC Design Challenges and Model Driven Engineering

Every two years, the semiconductor industry publishes the International Technology Roadmap for Semiconductors. The last edition [ITRS05] published in December 2005 looks at the challenges facing the industry until 2020. We will analyze below the identified needs in the SoC design domain that can be helped by model driven engineering.

6.2.1. *Cost*

The main message of the ITRS since 2003 has been that "Cost (of design) is the greatest threat to continuation of the semiconductor roadmap" (and so of Moore's law). The non-recurring engineering (NRE) costs of a product are divided between the manufacturing NRE costs that are on the order of millions of Euros and the NRE design costs that reach tens of millions of Euros. Further more a large portion of the designs fail due to errors detected too late in the design process. These NRE design costs are mainly the salaries of the engineers involved

Using software engineering techniques like model driven engineering is natural for the so-called power-efficient system-on-chip design because software development cost represents up to 80% of the overall development cost. Hardware manufacturing cost is no longer the main NRE cost for embedded systems. Design and even more test are getting exponentially more expensive. This is not a problem anymore; it has reached the crisis level!

6.2.2. *Silicon complexity*

The impact of process scaling on the design complexity mainly comes from two factors:

- Previously ignorable phenomena now have an impact at all levels of hardware design;

- Heterogeneity of the technologies (logic, memory, analog and mixed signal, micro/nano electromechanical systems, etc).

This complexity implies that the engineers have to be trained to several technologies to handle their interactions and that the tools have to take into account this new complexity. Large chips can no longer be considered as synchronous because of clock propagation delays or even defect free. We enter here the reign of fault-tolerant distributed systems with all the added complexity it represents.

6.2.3. *Productivity*

As systems get more and more complex (built from more and more transistors), the productivity of the design team has to increase to keep the cost and the development time in acceptable bounds. This increase in productivity has to be exponential to keep up with the exponential increase in integration density and the demand of new features in the products. The ITRS identifies several implied challenges: reuse, verification and test, cost-driven optimization, embedded software design, reliable implementation platforms and design process management.

Reuse is what software engineering is all about: functions, procedures, modules, components, models are all different forms of reusable units. In the domain of hardware design, reuse has also been a central idea going from small blocks to large blocks and now the so-called Intellectual Properties (IPs) which can be complete cores such as CPUs, DSPs, I/O units, etc. We will see below that a component based approach is central to most of the model driven contributions to SoC design.

Verification and test account for more than 70% the design time. It is therefore crucial to limit the need of costly simulations by developing correct by construction methodologies. Model transformations and automatic code generation can help in this domain to automatically derive lower level models and test cases. We also need as precise as possible semantics in the metamodels to allow such automatic code generation and also high-level (semi-)formal verification. Indeed the models at each level of abstraction should be verified against the higher level models. This is only possible if the models are non-ambiguous.

Cost driven optimization is a very complex issue because there are many different costs to take into account: manufacturing recurring costs, NRE costs (design and manufacturing), but also energy costs as many of the embedded systems are battery powered devices, and even environmental costs. Model driven techniques, by allowing to separate the concerns, can help to deal with this complexity but designing methodologies taking these problems into account is very challenging.

Embedded software design is becoming the principal issue. While UML is gaining ground in the industry, most of the embedded software is still designed in low level languages such as C or even assembly or macro assembly languages. Software engineering technologies need to be adapted to the particularities of the constrained embedded domain (mostly to real-time constraints) before being deployed in the industry. Co-design, meaning coupled and concurrent design of the hardware and software parts of the system, brings new problems. Partitioning (or mapping) the functionalities between software and hardware is a major issue in itself that needs to be supported by tools to enable an efficient design space exploration. Many hardware platforms exist today (OMAP [OMAP], Nexperia [Nexperia], STI cell [CELL]...). To allow the tools to support them efficiently and reliably, their number has to decrease and standards need to be defined. Some interoperability standards are currently being defined to help in this matter such as SPIRIT [SPIRIT], OCP [OCP03] or SystemC [SystemC].

There is also some variety of circuit fabrics to choose from. The EDA (Electronic Design Automation) tools have difficulties to provide reliable synthesis to such a variety. The level of automation has to increase even more to deal with the complexity of the systems and to hide to the designers the silicon complexity.

Design process management is in itself a big issue. Indeed, a design team needs various specialists (algorithm, software design, hardware design, software verification, hardware verification, system integrators, etc.) that are highly competent in the tools they use. The management problem comes when all these people from different backgrounds have to cooperate closely using often incompatible tools. The team needs a common language with agreed upon semantics in order to have a chance to succeed designing a product under the very high pressure of the reducing time-to-market window. Models may be an answer to this problem as they can be based on common metamodels and expressed as profiles of a single graphical language as UML. The profile standardization efforts currently going on at the OMG are a good step in this direction. These profiles will be presented briefly in section 6.3.

6.2.4. *Model Driven Engineering Assets*

Model driven engineering promotes the separation of concerns to enhance reuse. This separation can help design team members to do their particular job while sharing the same model or model set, each of them possibly having a different view on these models. The interfaces between the expertise domains can be well defined in the common model and each engineer can concentrate on its own domain. A particular separation that is at the heart of model driven engineering is the separation of the business and application logic from the underlying platform technology (from the Model Driven Architecture [MiJi03] approach of the OMG). This separation is crucial also in SoC design with the constant evolution of the manufacturing and simulation technologies.

Finally, the hardware industry has always tried to automate as much as possible the low level development stages with the EDA tools. It is thus natural for hardware engineers to automate code generation from higher level descriptions or models. The lowest manual level will thus rise upwards from the industry standard RTL to embrace TLM of even higher abstraction levels in the future. Model transformations can be the support for such automated code generation.

6.3. UML Profiles for SoC Design

The need for high level formalisms to help design embedded systems and particularly SoCs has given rise to several standardization initiatives at the OMG. These initiatives concern two domains: system modeling and analysis and electronic system level (ESL) modeling.

6.3.1. *Embedded System Modeling and Analysis*

Two concurrent profiles are under standardization: SysML [SysML06], the system modeling language and MARTE [MARTE05], the modeling and analysis of real-time and embedded systems profile. SysML is a generic system modeling language with no particular focus on embedded systems. It allows the designer to track the requirements along the modeling process and brings the paradigm of block diagrams to UML via a modification of the composite structure diagram of UML. It is presented in greater detail in Chapter 3.

The MARTE profile is targeted towards embedded systems. It will allow modeling both the application and the execution platform as well as the mapping of the application on the execution platform. It refines the time concepts of UML and the scheduling, performance and time (SPT) profile of UML 1.x, allowing modeling logical, discrete and continuous time models. The models will be annotatable with non-functional properties to express and analyze the various constraints the system is subjected to (real time, power consumption, various costs). An extension for modeling repetitive structures is also included in MARTE that will help to design the future regular architectures.

6.3.2. *Electronic System Level Modeling*

In the effort to raise the abstraction level for electronic modeling, the emerging abstraction is the so-called electronic system level (ESL). It is an abstraction level above the industry standard register transfer level (RTL) allowing much faster co-simulation of the software and the hardware of the system. It is actually a set of abstraction levels called transaction level modeling (TLM) where the communications are represented as read and write operations in memory while at the RT level, they are represented as signals propagating along wires. This allows speedups of hundreds to thousands of times.

Several languages compete at the ESL. The two main languages are SystemC [SystemC], based on C++, and System Verilog [SystemVerilog04], based on Verilog. Both languages expose nearly the same concepts, making it possible to express both the software and the execution platform by way of the modules communicating through channels of various semantics. They also include a simulation engine allowing cycle accurate simulation of the execution of the software running on the hardware.

At the OMG, the UML for SoC profile [UML4SoC05] is being standardized as a profile for ESL modeling. It is mainly based on the composite structure diagram and introduces the concepts needed to model hardware architectures at that level: modules, channels, ports and a few specializations of these, like clock and reset ports. It makes it possible to automatically generate skeletons of SystemC or equivalent languages. Another noteworthy profile is the UML for SystemC profile [RSRB05]. The approach is here to define in UML all that is needed to be able to automatically generate complete SystemC code, not only skeletons. Thus, all the concepts of the UML for SoC profile are present and there is also the possibility to define the behavior of the modules and the channels in a non ambiguous way. There is currently a tool specific implementation (for the code generation part) that is not considered for standardization.

A MDE approach for SoC co-modeling could be based on these profiles, starting from SysML for the earliest stages, then going to MARTE to analyze diverse properties and to partition the system between hardware and software, and finally using either the UML for SoC or the UML for SystemC profiles to help generate TLM (and even RTL) simulation code. We introduce in the next sections such an approach targeted to intensive signal processing applications.

6.4. MDE Approach to SoC Co-Modeling

The Model Driven Engineering (MDE) approach advocates the use of models at different levels of abstraction. A model represents an abstract view of the reality, it is defined by a metamodel specifying the available concepts. A common MDE development process is to start from a high level of abstraction and to go to a targeted model by flowing through intermediate levels of abstraction. Usually, the high level models contain only domain specific concepts, while technological concepts are introduced smoothly in the intermediate levels. The targeted levels are used for different purposes: code generation, simulation, verification, or as inputs to produce other models...

A key point of the MDE is the transformation between models. The transformations make it possible to go from one model at a given abstraction level to another model at another level, and to keep the different models synchronized. Related models are described by their metamodels, on which we can define some mapping rules describing how concepts from one metamodel are to be mapped on the concepts of the other metamodel. From these mapping rules we deduce the transformations between any models conforming to the metamodels.

The clear separation between the high level models and the technological models makes it easy to switch to a new technology while re-using the old designs. This may even be done automatically provided the right tool.

6.4.1. *Multiple Models in SoC*

SoC co-design asks for a strong interaction between people from different fields. This depends of course on the application domains, but this is also strongly characterized by the diversity of the know-how, where each job has its own background, concepts, languages and tools.

Embedded systems are fully specified by a set of interactions between hardware and software component units and have to react to the environment. SoCs can be considered as particular cases of embedded systems. SoC design covers a lot of different viewpoints including the application modeling by the aggregation of functional components, the assembly of existing physical components, the verification and the simulation of the modeled system, and the synthesis of a complete end-product integrated into a single chip. As a rule a SoC is a heterogeneous circuit including programmable processors, memory units, interconnection mechanisms and various hardware functional units (Digital Signal Processors, application specific circuits, I/O units, etc). These components can be generated for a particular application.

They can also be obtained from IP (Intellectual Property) providers. The ability to re-use software or hardware components is without any doubt a major asset for a co-design environment.

The multiplicity of the abstraction levels can be appropriately handled by a model driven approach. The information is used with a different viewpoint for each abstraction level. This information is defined only once in a single model. The links or transformation rules between the abstraction levels allow the re-use of the concepts for a different purpose.

6.4.2. *Metamodels for the "Y" Design*

Metamodeling brings a set of tools which will enable us to specify our *application* and *hardware architecture* models using UML tools, to reuse functional and physical IPs, to ensure refinements between abstraction levels via mapping rules, to ensure interoperability between the different abstraction levels used in a same codesign, and to ensure, through the use of standards, the opening to other tools, like verification tools.

Our proposal is partially based upon the concepts of the "Y-chart" [GaKu83] . The MDE contributes to express the model transformations which correspond to successive refinements between the abstraction levels. The original proposal focuses on the Intensive Signal Processing (ISP), enabling us to restrict the application domain and to provide a complete MDE approach from the high level designer's to the code generation. The scope is now widened by the use of new standards like MARTE and SysML. MARTE is defined in collaboration with ours partners.

6.4.3. *From High Level Models*

The *application* and *hardware architecture* are described by different metamodels. Some concepts from these two metamodels are similar in order to unify and so simplify their understanding and use. Models for application and hardware architecture may be done separately (maybe by two different teams). At this point, it becomes possible to map the application model on the hardware architecture model. For this purpose we introduce a third metamodel, called an association metamodel, to express associations between the functional components and the hardware components. This metamodel imports the two previously presented metamodels. It also enables the expression of the scheduling, and refactoring of the model through the execution of a refactoring tool.

The abstract syntax of the application and the hardware architecture are described by different metamodels. These metamodels share common structures in order to simplify their understanding and use.

They share a common modeling paradigm, the component oriented approach, to ease reusability. Reusability is one of the key points to face the time to market challenge that the conception of embedded systems implies. In both *application* and *architecture*, components propose an interface materialized by their ports. The interfaces make it possible to encapsulate the structure and behavior of the components, and make them independent of their environment.

The three metamodels are now based on the MARTE and SysML profiles. They share common construction mechanisms, like components, and concepts to express repetitive constructs in a compact way [CuDeMa05]. This kind of repetitive constructs are well adapted to Intensive Signal Processing which is our primary target, and are more understandable for a compiler or an optimization tool.

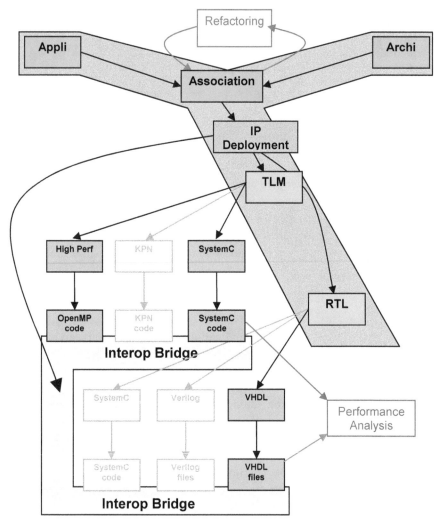

Figure 6.1. *Metamodels for the "Y" design*

6.4.4. *To Technology Models*

All the previously defined models, *application*, *architecture* and *association*, are independent from any technology. Components have no knowledge of the execution, simulation or synthesis technology. Such technology knowledge (Java, SystemC RTL, SystemC TLM, VHDL, etc.) is introduced in the *deployment* model. Once all the components are associated with some technology, the deployment is realized. From this point, automatic transformations can generate intermediate models and targeted models. 0 shows the Transaction Level Model (TLM) metamodel, and the Register Transfer Level (RTL) metamodel used as intermediate metamodels. More intermediate levels (not shown) can be generated. These models can be used by tools to perform different tasks like verification, simulation, refactoring, etc.

The diversity of the technologies requires interoperability between abstraction levels, simulation and synthesis languages. For this purpose we define an *interoperability* metamodel which makes it possible to model interfaces between technologies. The corresponding model can be automatically generated from the *deployment* model. We use a trace of the transformations for this purpose [BoBoDe05].

Mapping rules between the *deployment* metamodel, and *interoperability* and *technology* metamodels can be defined to automatically specialize the *deployment* model to the chosen technologies. From each of the resulting models we could automatically produce the execution/simulation code and the interoperability infrastructure.

The simulation results can lead to a refinement of the *application*, of the *hardware architecture*, of the *association* or of the *deployment* models. The stages of design could be:

- Separate application and hardware architecture modeling;

- Association with semi-automatic mapping and scheduling;

- Deployment (choice of simulation or execution level and platform for each component);

- Automatic generation of the various platform specific simulation or execution models;

- Automatic simulation or code generation;

- Refinement of the top level models according to the simulation results.

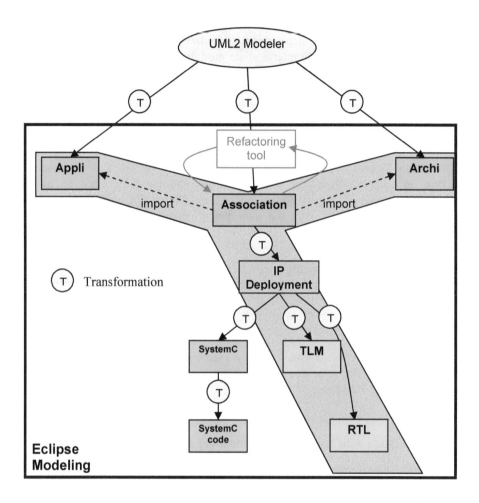

Figure 6.2. *Soc Development Process with Gaspard2*

6.5. Gaspard2 Development Environment

MDE implies adapted tooling to automate, as much as possible, SoC design. Tools must be studied to get a homogeneous, user-friendly and powerful environment. Here, we present the Gaspard2 Development Environment, a MDE tool that includes concepts of transformations through metamodels for SoC co-modeling. It respects the Gaspard metamodel architecture, as described in Figure 6.2.

6.5.1. *Simplify the work with good tools*

While creating a framework it is important to think about which tools are needed to ease implementation maintenance and reuse. Because the framework has to work on all platforms, we have chosen JAVA for its portability and its powerful built-in libraries. For writing code, we need a good graphic development tool. We have thought of the Eclipse workbench [Eclipse] which is used more and more to develop in JAVA. Furthermore, Eclipse has many important and useful features that have significantly directed our choice. It offers the advantage to add plug-ins with a very complete library that let us setup and overload all the workbench features. Moreover, a big community of developers constantly adds plug-ins for this tool. We have found a homogeneous system to develop our tools in the form of a plug-in.

Gaspard2 is a suite of transformations of models through metamodels. We thus have to use a tool to create and manage our metamodels that can be easily integrated to Eclipse. We have chosen the Eclipse Modeling Framework (EMF) [Emf03]. It is a part of the Eclipse project and works like an Eclipse plug-in. EMF uses Ecore, a metamodeling language based on EMOF, to write metamodels, then, it generates a complete and customizable Eclipse plug-in framework in which we can create our models with a simple treelike editor.

There are only a few model-to-model transformations tools, e.g. Kermeta [Kermeta]. In general, these tools don't have enough complex and structured language elements to describe our transformation algorithms. Model-to-text transformation tools like MOFScript [MofScript] can not be easily extended to transform to a target model. These softwares perform transformations to text files, generally source code to be compiled. Technically, the engine should be an Eclipse plug-in with an access to EMF models and metamodels. So, we have decided to use our in house tool, ModTransf, which corresponds to all these points. The last version under development of ModTransf is available as an Eclipse plug in which allows a simple access to EMF metamodels.

6.5.2. *Transformation Engine: ModTransf*

Model to model transformations are at the heart of the MDE approach. Anyone wishing to use MDE in its projects is sooner or later facing the question of how to perform the model transformations. Today the OMG QVT standardization process is complete [QVT05] and transformation tools become available, but this was not always the case, and to fulfill the lack of tools at the early days of MDE, we have developed ModTransf, a simple yet powerful transformation engine. Based on the different QVT proposals and on our needs, we have identified the following requirements for the transformation engine:

- Multiple models as inputs and outputs;

- Different kinds of models: MOF and JMI based, EMF, XML with schema based, or graph of objects;

- Simple to use;

- Easy modification of the rules to follow metamodel evolutions;

- Hybrid: Imperative and declarative rules;

- Inheritance for the rules;

- Reversible rules when possible;

- Customizable, in order to perform experimentations;

- Code generation;

- Free and Open-Source.

The proposed solution fulfills all these needs: ModTransf is a rule based engine taking one or more models as inputs and producing one or more models as outputs. The rules can be declarative as well as imperative. They can be expressed in two different manners: in XML, with a graphical tree editor, or using a UML like graphical syntax. A transformation is done by submitting a concept to the engine. The engine then searches the most appropriate transformation rule for this concept and applies it to produce the corresponding result concept(s). The rule describes how properties of the input concept should be mapped, after a transformation, to the properties of the output concept.

The code generation follows the same principle, but the output concept creation is replaced by code generation performed with a template mechanism. A rule specifies one or more templates to use, and each template contains holes replaced by the values of the input concepts.

The ModTransf engine is an Open Source project available on our website [ModTransf06].

6.5.3. *From UML2 Modelers to the Gaspard2 Environment*

The first step is to model a Gaspard2 model with a graphical interface to be user friendly. As shown on top of 0, models are made with third-party UML2 Modelers, using the Gaspard2 profile. For the moment, we provide a profile for the MagicDraw UML modeling software [MD06]. The model is then transformed in the UML2 metamodel of EMF [Emf03], exporting the used profile elements at the same time. This intermediate model factorizes a number of complex model-to-model transformations that we have to do. This model relies on an EMF internal format, easier to read and to transform. It is taken as an input by the Gaspard2 environment and transformed on the fly in the Gaspard2 metamodel.

The Gaspard2 top-level metamodel is broken into 3 metamodels. The application metamodel gives an abstract representation of an application. The architecture metamodel abstracts the hardware execution platform. The association metamodel imports both of them and makes it possible to express distribution and scheduling relations between application model elements and architecture model elements. The separation of the application, hardware execution platform and association models enhances the reuse of the model capabilities. The association model is the entry point for the other transformations in the Gaspard2 transformation flow.

6.5.4. Model Refactoring and Deployment Metamodel

The association model describes a possibly partial distribution and scheduling of the application onto the execution hardware architecture. Distribution and scheduling algorithms can be used to compute or complete the association. Such transformations are called refactoring transformations because they are modifications of a model with respect to the same metamodel. They are implemented by direct model manipulations through the metamodel specific application programming interface generated by EMF.

After that, a transformation is made from the association model to the deployment model. In this last model, the user decides which language at which abstraction level using which library component will be the target of the simulation or execution code automatic generation.

All the resources needed for the code generation have to be indicated explicitly or implicitly in this model. After this all the transformations are fully automated to generate the set of models respecting the metamodels of the chosen targets and the interoperability model that are finally used to generate the simulation or execution code.

6.5.5. *Example of Concept Transformation*

The successive transformations make it possible to progressively transforming the high-level constructs into lower level equivalent constructs closer and closer to code generation. We give below an example of such a chain of transformations.

In the 3 top-level models, repetition is represented by pattern-based access in arrays. This abstraction (inspired by the Array-OL language [DeLa+95]) is well suited to represent data-parallel computations, repetitive hardware units such as grids and regular mappings as can be found in data parallel languages for distributed memory computers (High Performance Fortran for example).

At the TLM level, the hardware has to be expanded to the individual components in order to evaluate the resource access conflicts and the data-parallel tasks are distributed to the individual components. The representation of these sets of tasks is converted from a combination of pattern-based accesses represented by a set of matrices to polyhedra. In the lower level model enabling the generation of the simulation code, the polyhedra are converted to loop nests enumerating their points by the way of the Chunky Loop Generator (CLooG) library [CLG02].

For example, let us consider a 2×2 processors grid. We want to distribute a 10×10 array of tasks to these 4 processors in a cyclic way. The high level matrix-based representation is converted to a parameterized polyhedron given by the following set of equations:

$$\{x=2i+px,\ y=2j+py,\ 0\leq x<10,\ 0\leq y<10,\ 0\leq i<5,\ 0\leq j<5,\ 0\leq px<1,\ 0\leq py<1\},$$

where $(px,\ py)$ is the processor location on the grid, $(x,\ y)$ the current task to execute and $(i,\ j)$ the local index of the task. This polyhedron is then given to CLooG that produces the C like loops of 0 where S represents the task to execute on a given processor.

```
for( x=px; x<=9; x++) {

      for( y=py; y<=9; y++) {

            if(( x-px )%2 == 0) {

                  i = (x-px)/2 ;

                  if( (y-py)%2 == 0) {

                        j = (y-py)/2 ;

                        S ;

                  }

            }

      }
}
```

Figure 6.3. *C like code for the polyhedron points enumeration generated by the GlooG library*

6.5.6. *Evolution of our environment*

The Gaspard2 Development Environment is a research prototyping platform and thus is subject to evolution. Adding a metamodel in the flow "only" requires defining the model transformations from the above models and to the lower models. It is, of course, possible to add new compilation targets as, for instance, a target that directly generates formal verification code to be used by an external tool.

Another interesting procedure is to include a graphical modeler into the Gaspard framework in order to be fully independent from external modelers. A good way to add such an interface is by using the Graphic Editing Framework (GEF), which works well with EMF as explained in [MoGeWa04].

6.6. Conclusion

We have shown in this chapter how the model driven engineering could help for embedded system design, especially for systems-on-chip co-design. We have first stressed the need for a dramatic increase of the design team's productivity due to a superexponential increase in the design complexity. We have then presented the current standardization efforts in this area and sketched a model driven approach for intensive signal processing co-modeling. We have finally explained how such a framework is implemented using the eclipse modeling framework and the ModTransf model transformation tool. We think that there is a great potential for model driven techniques in this area given the need for automation, the focus on reuse and the complexity of the domain.

6.7. References

[BBC+05] L. BONDE, P. BOULET, A. CUCCURU, J.-L. DEKEYSER, C. DUMOULIN, P. MARQUET, S. MEFTALI and M. SAMYN, Model Driven Engineering for Distributed Embedded Real-Time Systems, chapter in *Model Driven Architecture for Intensive Embedded Systems*. ISTE, August 2005.

[BoBoDe05] Lossan BONDE, Pierre BOULET, and Jean-Luc DEKEYSER, "Traceability and interoperability at different levels of abstraction in model transformations". In *Forum on Specification and Design Languages, FDL'05*, Lausanne, Switzerland, September 2005.

[CELL] IBM Research, Cell Architecture, http://www.research.ibm.com/cell

[CLG02] C. BASTOUL, *Generating loops for scanning polyhedra*, PRiSM, Versailles University, 2002.

[CuDeMa05] Arnaud CUCCURU, Jean-Luc DEKEYSER, Philippe MARQUET, and Pierre BOULET, "Towards UML 2 extensions for compact modeling of regular complex topologies - A partial answer to the MARTE RFP". In *MoDELS/UML 2005, ACM/IEEE 8th International Conference on Model Driven Engineering Languages and Systems*, pages 445–459, Montego Bay, JamaicaLecture Notes in Computer Science vol. 3713, October 2005.

[DeLa+95] Alain DEMEURE, A. LAFARGE, E. BOUTILLON, D. ROZZONELLI, J.-C DUFOURD, and J.-L MARRO, "Array-OL : Proposition d'un formalisme tableau pour le traitement de signal multi-dimensionnel", In Gretsi, Juan-Les-Pins, France, September 1995.

[Eclipse] Eclipse Platform, http://www.eclipse.org/

[Emf03] Catherine GRIFFIN, *Using EMF*, IBM Corp., http://www.eclipse.org, may 2003.

[GaKu83] D. D. GAJSKI and R. KUHN, "Guest editor introduction: New VLSI-tools, *IEEE Computer*, vol. 16, no. 12, pp. 11–14, Dec. 1983.

[ITRS05] International Technology Roadmap for Semiconductors, DesignEdition. http://www.itrs.net/Common/2005ITRS/Design.pdf, 2005.

[Kermeta] Triskell team, Kermeta Modeling Language, http://www.kermeta.org.

[MARTE05] ProMARTE Working Group, *MARTE Initial Submission*, OMG Document realtime/05-11-01, http://www.omg.org/cgibin/doc?realtime/2005-11-01

[MD06] NoMagic, *MagicDraw UML*, http://www.magicdraw.com.

[MiJi03] Joaquin MILLER and Jishnu MUKERJI, Eds., *MDA Guide (Draft Version 0.2)*, {http://www.omg.org/docs/ab/03-01-03.pdf}, 2003.

[ModTransf06] Cédric DUMOULIN, "ModTransf: A model to model transformation engine," http://www.lifl.fr/west/modtransf, 2006.

[MofScript] SINTEF's development community, *The MOFScript Language*, MODELWARE project, http://www.eclipse.org/gmt/mofscript.

[MoGeWa04] B. MOORE, D. DEAN, A. GERBER, G. WAGENKNECHT and P. VANDERHEYDEN, *Eclipse Development using the Graphical Editing Framework and the Eclipse Modeling Framework*, IBM Corp., www.ibm/redbooks, February 2004.

[OCP03] OCP International Partnership, *Open Core Protocol Specification 2.0*, http://www.ocpip.org/, 2003.

[OMAP] Texas Instruments, OMAP Platform, http://focus.ti.com/docs/general/omap2homepage.tsp

[OMG06] Object Management Group, Ed., *(UML 2.0): Superstructure Draft Adopted Specification*, http://www.omg.org/cgi-bin/doc?ptc/03-07-06/, July 2003.

[Nexperia] Philips, Nexperia, http://www.semiconductors.philips.com/products/nexperia/

[QVT05] MOF QVT final adopted specification, OMG document, ptc/05-11-01, 2005.

[RSRB05] E. RICCOBENE, P. SCANDURRA, A. ROSTI, S. BOCCHIO, *A UML 2.0 Profile for SystemC : Towards High-Level SoC Design*, Proceedings of the ACM International Conference on Embedded Software, 2005.

[SPIRIT] SPIRIT Consortium, Structure for Packaging, Integrating and Re-using IP within Tool-flows, http://www.spiritconsortium.com/

[SystemC] Open SystemC Initiative, *The SystemC Library*, http://www.systemc.org.

[SysML06] SysML Merge Team, *SysML Specification v. 1.0 (draft)*, OMG document ad/06-03-01, http://www.omg.org/cgi-bin/doc?ad/06-03-01, 2006.

[SystemVerilog04] Accellera Organization, Inc., *SystemVerilog 3.1a Language Reference Manual*, 2004, http://www.eda.org/sv/

[UML4SoC05] Object Management Group, Ed., *UML Extension Profile for SoC RFC*, 2005, OMG document realtime/05-03-01, http://www.omg.org/cgi-bin/doc?realtime/2005-03-01, 2005.

CHAPTER 7

Schedulability Analysis and MDD

Chapter written by S. Rouxel, G. Gogniat, J-P. Diguet, J-L. Philippe and C. Moy

IRISA / INRIA Rennes L.E.S.T.E.R. CNRS FRE 2734
SCEE Group, SUPELEC
University Research Laboratory, France
Cesson-Sévigné France
{rouxel, gogniat, diguet, philippe}@univ-ubs.fr
christophe.moy@rennes.supelec.fr

7.1. Introduction

Complex system-on-a-chip (SOC) challenge is now achievable since both required hardware resources and integration technologies are available. The telecom domain is an interesting example where the SOC paradigm already enables the design of multi-standard chips (e.g. GSM, IEEE 802.11, IS-95). Such an evolution promotes the software radio concept for the management of multiple standards [MIT 95] [SDR 06]. However, the design of these systems based on heterogeneous platforms (e.g. DSP, FPGA, GPP) and intensive-computation software applications (e.g. encryption, scrambling algorithm, service management) can no longer be addressed using traditional CAD tools. Actually higher levels of abstraction are required to cope with the design complexity and to provide the designers with an early feedback. Such co-design tools partly exist and are based on scalable hardware and software IPs reuse. Some of these tools can already meet the design constraints, like CoWare, which uses SystemC/C++ hardware language specifications, or Co-fluent studio, which is based on the MCSE methodology [BOL 97] [CAL 90].

In this chapter we will stress how our solution offers a simple and more unified way to fill the gap between the specification and the prototyping phases, through an UMTS transceiver case study.

Major projects related to software radio are described in UML which enables modeling systems through a graphical approach. Furthermore, UML continuously evolves to consider new specific characteristics from different activity domains thanks to the development of new profiles. A profile specializes the UML language for a work context, which offers scalability. It specifies all characteristics (e.g. elements for real-time application) and relations between the UML elements. It allows model-based *a priori* verifications. A designer relies on the profile to analyze, generate code and specify various application and architecture constraints. Moreover, dependencies, inheritance, or groupings between profiles can be performed to promote the reuse of domain specific needs. Regarding the software radio application, three profiles are of interest: UML profile for software radio [SRP 05], UML profile for schedulability performance and time [SPP 03] and UML profile for QoS and fault tolerance [QFP 05]. Each profile provides some specific characteristics that are useful to perform the evaluation of the system performances. Dealing with these profiles, a system can theoretically be accurately specified by integrating various constraint types (e.g. power consumption, bounded execution time).

However, the standardization of these profiles is not always completed and existing profiles do not cover all the parameters required for system prototyping. Here we propose to improve these different profiles through the development of a new and specific one. Its purpose is to stress standard concepts required for prototyping and to add hardware attributes that are not currently taken into account. Furthermore, the goal of our project (A3S project) is not limited to the definition of the A3S profile but also targets its implementation within a rapid-prototyping tool to evaluate the feasibility of complex applications over heterogeneous platforms (with DSP, FPGA components). Specification of dynamic reconfiguration is also investigated since this feature will be mandatory, especially for software radio applications.

The remainder of this chapter is as follows. Section 7.2 presents various high level specifications for system prototyping. Section 7.3 provides a global approach of system modeling as promoted within our project. Section 7.4 details the UML modeling by giving the set of parameters required to compute verifications and performance evaluation. Section 7.5 details the scheduling analysis techniques used to realize the performance evaluation. Section 7.6 gives an example of an UMTS application modeling. Section 7.7 concludes the chapter.

7.2. Related Work

Many tools aim at modeling systems, performing verifications, simulations, validations, and synthesis. Different modeling styles with different granularities are considered, different input specification languages as C, SystemC, VHDL, are also used to validate, verify, simulate or emulate a system [SHU 03] [EDW 97]. First co-design tools like VULCAN were using simple and limited hardware architecture models, while others like COSYMA were based on dedicated hardware co-processors to speed up software execution [GUP 93] [ERN 93]. COWARE and PTOLEMY consider heterogeneous specifications to respectively design specific applications (embedded telecommunication) and co-simulate heterogeneous HW/SW systems [DAV 01].

However, these approaches are limited as they require the use of different tools that must be kept updated. Actually the goal is to perform both modeling and design specification of hardware platforms and software applications within a single tool and through a common language to be less dependent of multiple software update [ARA 99]. The SoC Environment (SCE) developed within the University of California, Irvine provides such an approach as the design specification in each stage of the design flow is defined through a SpecC code [GAJ 04]. However, the use of a generic language, common to different domains, that is flexible enough to model all co-design aspects (e.g. architectural and application specifications, component properties, constraints specification) would be interesting. To target such a philosophy, the most recent rapid prototyping tools integrate methodology of hardware-software co-design into the concept of MDD (Model Driven Development) through UML. MOCCA and GASPARD v02 in the DART project describe their models in UML [FRO 04] [DAR 03]. The MOCCA model compiler for reconfigurable architecture requires an action language to define low-level behavior. The DART project focuses on limited application domain (intensive signal processing application) and performs some transformations from the UML model to specific ISP UML. Indeed, UML provides elements to real time specification needs (e.g. parallelism, behavior, concurrency, communication modeling). Arguing that UML is incomplete [LAV 02], the SysML (System Modeling Language) project tries to add extensions of UML to integrate hardware aspects in response to OMG request for proposal [SYS 03].

We propose to use a unique language from specification to validation. Our approach relies on our UML A3S profile that inherits from other standardized profiles and completes them. This profile improves and offers more hardware specification possibilities that are essential for software radio or other electronic systems in order to specify hardware and software architecture systems. In addition, our high abstraction level specification alleviates the modeling and the validation of applications that belong to other specific application domains. Moreover, as we consider applications as a set of IPs, components are only characterized by non-functional parameters instead of source codes (which depend on their implementation and need different tools).

7.3. Global Approach

A3S approach proposes a UML software framework where the designer can rapidly and easily prototype his system and check if constraints are met in terms of timing, memory, area, and power consumption. The main steps of our design flow for virtual prototyping are depicted in Figure 7.1.

7.3.1. *Application Specification (1st step)*

With the MDA approach, software applications and hardware architectures can be specified independently, so 1st step and 2nd step (see Figure 7.1) can be exchanged. To manage complexity, an application is split into several functions that are represented by independent generic software (SW) components. It corresponds to a PIM (Platform Independent Model) since each function can be potentially mapped onto any hardware component. These SW components have specific non-functional parameters that correspond to specification constraints coming from the application or from designer requests. One example of these parameters is the periodicity of the SW component which is independent from any implementation. More information about these parameters is detailed in section 7.4. At this stage of the design flow, SW components can represent any function.

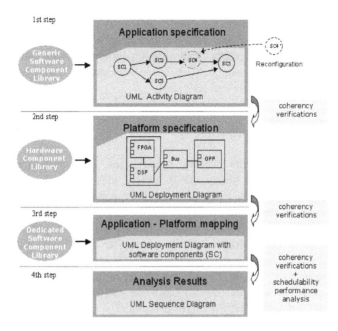

Figure 7.1. *A3S design flow*

The application is modeled through a functional scheme based on the UML activity diagram which is composed of a set of action states (SW components) and transitions. Transitions correspond to dependency relations between functions and have specific parameters related to the exchanged data (e.g. number, size). For each component, the designer specifies the corresponding parameters values.

An activity diagram example for an UMTS-FDD receiver is given in Figure 7.2. This diagram also addresses the links between the different SW components to specify the system radio functionality. The black dot represents the input of the application which takes place at the propagation channel side. Each arrow corresponds to an edge (transition) and represents a data-flow dependency. The UMTS-FDD receiver is mainly a data-flow application with periodic and iterative functions (FrameProcessing, SlotProcessing, RadioProcessing, TransportBloc). The black dot in the circle is the output of the application; it corresponds to the exchanged data between the physical layer and the higher layers of the OSI model.

Through this model the designer can easily replace, add, move/remove a SW component, or modify some parameters to enhance the algorithm and thus test various configurations. By this way, he can analyze the impact of different reconfigurations, which is of major importance in a software radio context. Once the application model is completed, some coherency constraints verifications are performed. Among them, the tool verifies that all connections between SW components have been correctly done, through compatible data format and that all required parameters have been settled. These verifications have been implemented within the Objecteering case tool [OBJ 06].

7.3.2. Platform Specification (2nd step)

This step deals with the platform specification. Each hardware component is described in a hardware library (DSP, FPGA, GPP, memory, interconnect and ASIC) corresponding to an UML package. Each component has specific attributes defined through its stereotypes (this point is developed in section 7.4). The designer builds his platform by assembling hardware components instantiations (in UML sense) through a UML deployment diagram. Many hardware platforms can be realized, especially heterogeneous platforms. This kind of architecture is essential for telecommunication applications like software radio that need flexibility (offered by FPGA and DSP components for hardware and software reconfiguration) and important computation resources (multi-processor).

7.3.3. Application – Platform Mapping (3rd step)

After the software application and hardware platform modeling steps are completed, the designer chooses which dedicated SW component is implemented onto which hardware component. For each SW component, the designer selects the corresponding function in the software component library since a SW component corresponds to a processing element that is not dedicated to a specific target. Thus, the function represents an implementation of the SW component on a processor (e.g. DSP, GPP), a FPGA or an ASIC. The target hardware component selected to implement the SW component is obtained by defining an instance of a hardware component within the hardware platform in the UML deployment diagram.

A broad range of implementation solutions can then be tested for a specific platform (PSM – Platform Specific Model) due to all possible combinations. The example in Figure 7.3 depicts a hardware platform composed of two DSPs (DSP_A, DSP_C) on which different software components are implemented (e.g. scrambling function is implemented on DSP_A). Thus the deployment diagram is refined by a software component instantiation implemented into a hardware component instantiation. This partitioning is performed through links between the software components from the UML activity diagram and the hardware components from the UML deployment diagram. For example, the DSP_A that is connected to DSP_C via FIFO_AC handles four functions (SCR, SUM, SPRdpcch, DPCCHctrl).

During the application specification step, non-functional verifications are automatically performed by the use of meta-model.

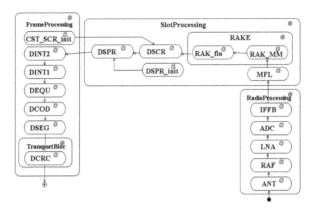

Figure 7.2. *UMTS-FDD Receiver Activity Diagram*

7.3.4. *Analysis results (4th step)*

Results are provided through a schematic view defined in a UML sequence diagram which is close to a Gantt diagram. The results emphasize the performances achieved by a heterogeneous platform with multi-processor resources to perform the application. For example, execution time, resources use rate, system evolution (scheduling), and allocated memory resources are exhibited. Scheduling information is very important as if the system cannot be scheduled or if it does not reach the required timing constraints, the solution is not relevant.

If the solution built does not satisfy the constraints, it is easy to modify the implementation choices just by modifying the links between software and hardware components in the UML activity diagram without modifying the diagram. As several applications and platforms can be specified it enables testing an application on different platforms and with different implementations for a same platform. It also promotes testing different configurations and re-configurations of the system. It is also possible to modify some hardware characteristics by changing hardware component parameters values. Moreover, the A3S CAD tool returns results that help designer to make modifications according to identified critical functions.

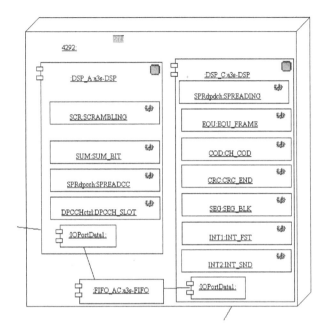

Figure 7.3. *Deployment diagram after mapping*

As the previous steps, coherency verifications are performed to check the solution. After this step, the system is completely specified and a functional analysis can be launched (presented in section 7.4).

7.4. UML Modeling

7.4.1. *Attributes identification*

During the application and platform specification steps, the designer provides the values of the software and the hardware component attributes to perform the coherency verification and analysis of the system. Each component (software and hardware) can be characterized into three parts as described in Figure 7.4. The first part concerns the non-functional characteristics (attributes) of the component.

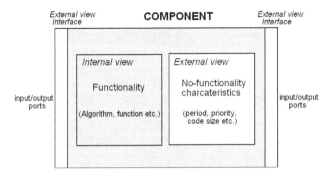

Figure 7.4. *Component Views*

For software components it represents the temporal aspects of the function (e.g. period) and the data characteristics. The second part describes its interface (its I/O port) with significant attributes relative to exchanged signal. The third part is relative to the functionality of the component. For hardware components it corresponds for example to the clock frequency, the type and quantity of internal/external memories. This view mainly corresponds to specification constraints. As our approach relies on IP cores, the internal view of the component is not explicitly represented since we assume that IP cores functional behavior (i.e. C, C++, SystemC, VHDL) is validated through other means that are outside the scope of this chapter. In our case attributes can be provided using the IP characteristics.

UML stereotypes make it possible to identify and characterize any elements by assigning different parameters called "attribute". So each element of UML can be specialized by using different stereotypes that are used to define component parameters. Generic SW components which compose the UML activity diagram, HW components, ports of HW components, dedicated SW component, ports of dedicated SW components have different stereotypes, which give them specific attributes. Basically, generic SW components which are not yet implemented have different attributes (e.g. a function is periodic or not, it has an initialization part or not) which correspond to a dedicated SW component which represents one implemented choice of one generic SW component. Each implementation choice brings some specific constraints that are highlighted through the non-functional attributes. They deal with function periodicity, execution time, size code of IP cores, priority level if a RTOS is used, and other attributes like data and code localization, and access memory types. HW components have different stereotypes to differentiate HW processing components (e.g. DSP, ASIC, GPP), memory components (e.g. FIFO, RAM, ROM), reconfigurable components (FPGA) with their associated ports, and communication components (e.g. bus, wire). Specific performance parameters are considered according to the hardware components (e.g. frequency, data/program memory size, port type, data width, throughput).

All identified parameters are required to perform an analysis. They are used during the scheduling analysis step, to compute resources use rates, to perform constraints verification and to check the coherency of the system.

7.4.2. Analysis details

Once specification and mapping have been completed and coherency verifications have been performed (i.e. no error about HW/SW connections, all attributes settled), the A3S tool generates a XML file gathering the information about the system. The file contains the diagrams (activity, deployment), the hardware/software components allocated, and the attribute values. More precisely the UML activity diagram that represents the functional application scheme of the system is encompassed in the XML file. Thanks to an XML parser this diagram is converted into a task graph. Thus, the parsing of this file makes it possible to build a General Task Graph (GTG) based on the Radha Ratan model since we consider the corresponding method to perform period derivation [DAS 99]. This method computes the period of each task within the GTG even if some tasks are previously unknown. The GTG nodes represent tasks (functions), and the GTG oriented edges are channels from producers (tasks) to consumers (tasks). Each task can be triggered by a data or a control. Each edge contains producer and consumer information corresponding to data/control to be exchanged between functions. For applications that use multi-processors, the choice of a function implementation can lead to additional communication tasks (in case of two tasks communicating and implemented on different hardware devices). The period derivation step is performed to compute the timing constraints (periods) that have not been settled by the designer during the specification steps. This point is important, since this kind of computation is very error prone and can be efficiently done with our CAD tool.

The GTG obtained from the XML processing is then used with the HW architecture characteristics within our real time analysis tool RTDT [TMA 04]. This tool performs automatically complex scheduling verification and provides performance analysis results which help the designer to drive his choices. Such automatic bridges and tools are essential to improve time to market and the quality of systems design.

7.5. Real time analysis tool (RTDT)

7.5.1. *Real time scheduling strategy*

7.5.1.1. *Task classification*

Usually, real-time embedded systems require a simple and safe scheduler which can guarantee that critical aperiodic or periodic tasks meet their deadlines. For these reasons, a static HPF (High Priority First) scheduling policy has been adopted, where the fixed priorities are computed as the inverse of the task period. The worst case response time is computed with an exact analysis [JOS 86].

In a first approach we consider two kinds of tasks. The first category is composed by the periodic tasks that are scheduled by means of hard real-time constraints (RTC), and sporadic tasks with hard RTC. Like in [DAV 98], we consider the sporadic tasks as periodic tasks with a period equals to the minimum delay between two subsequent executions; this value is provided by the Radha Ratan tool [DAS 99]. The second category includes the non critical sporadic tasks which are handled by a server task with the lowest priority that can be fixed by the designer. The task priority is computed as the inverse of the task period.

The question of multi-rate dependencies is solved by shifting the release time computation as detailed in [AZZ 02].

7.5.1.2. *Response time computation*

The exact response time is computed iteratively with the following equation:

$$\forall T_j \in HP(i), \exists R_i \leq D_i \, / \, R_i = \left(C_i + R_i \right) + \sum_{j \in HP(i)} \left\lceil \frac{R_i}{P_j} \right\rceil \times \left(C_j + C_{sw} \right) \qquad [7.1]$$

Where:

- *HP(i)*: is the set of tasks with higher priority comparing to task *i*;
- R_i: is the worst case response time of task *i*;
- D_i: is the execution deadline for task *i*,
- C_i: is the execution time of task *i*;
- B_i: is the longest time that task *i* can be delayed by lower priority tasks;
- P_j: is the period of task *j*;
- C_{sw}: is the context switching; $C_{sw} = \delta_0 + \sum_k \delta(k)$ [7.2]

With:

- δ_0: is the context switching overhead without any coprocessor,
- $\delta(k)$: is the overhead due to the coprocessor k.

The context switching overhead is the delay between the preemption of a given task and the activation of another task. The difficulty is that C_{sw} depends not only on the target processor and on the RTOS and its configuration but also on the number of tasks in the system and on the number of coprocessors. The influence of the number of tasks is not insignificant but can be neglected compared with the coprocessor context saving influence. Moreover, without the coprocessor, the available overhead metric is usually an average value estimated with different task sets. The influence of the coprocessor is obviously related to the number of data and status registers.

7.5.2. Design space exploration for HW/SW partitioning

7.5.2.1. Cost function

The cost function takes into account the global area of the SOC and its energy consumption. At a high level of abstraction, only relative estimations can be used for SW and HW IPs and the cost function is used to guide the selection of a reduced set of solutions. In order to eliminate solutions, relative costs are used to evaluate the cost value for a given schedulable solution S:

$$Cost(S) = \alpha \frac{Area(S) - MinArea}{MinArea} + \beta \frac{Pw(S) - MinPw}{MinPw} \qquad [7.3]$$

with $\alpha + \beta = 1$ and where *MinArea* is the schedulable solution with the minimal area without any power consideration and *MinPw* the schedulable solution with the minimal power without any area consideration. Note that the area cost influences the power consumption through the static power evaluation. So, the α parameter also acts on the power optimization.

7.5.2.2. Area Cost

The area cost includes the data and code memory size for software implementations, the area of coprocessors that can be shared by various tasks, the area of hardware accelerators and finally the area of memories added for communications.

7.5.2.3. *Power Cost*

The model for power evaluation is much more complex. Firstly, the dynamic power consumption depends on the SOC activity, which is strongly related to the task scheduling and switching. Secondly, the evolution of VLSI technology shows that static power consumption [BUT 00], especially in FPGAs, can no longer be neglected. Finally, in mobile embedded systems the important metric is the system lifespan. It means that the energy used must be optimized. However, in our context of periodic tasks the energy optimization is equivalent to the average power minimization over the hyper period. Our power model for an implementation S is given by:

$$Pw(S) = Pw_d + Pw_s \qquad [7.4]$$

where Pw_d is the average dynamic power dissipated during a hyper period T_G and Pw_s is the average static power.

7.5.2.4. *Dynamic power/energy metric*

Let Pw_d, the average dynamic power dissipated during a hyper period T_G.

$$Pw_d = \frac{E_d}{T_G} \qquad [7.5]$$

$$E_d = E_d(sw) + E_d(hw)$$

//E_d: energy consumed during a hyper period T_G $\qquad [7.6]$

$$E_d(sw) = E_d(idle) + E_d(switch) + E_d(exe) \qquad [7.7]$$

$$E_d(exe) = T_G \sum_{i \in sw} P_{wd}(i) \frac{C_i}{P_i} \quad //P_{wd}(i): \text{average power for task } i \qquad [7.8]$$

$$E_d(switch) = Pwd(switch)T_G \sum_{i \in sw} \frac{C_{sw}}{P_i}$$

//$P_{wd}(switch)$: average task switching power   [7.9]

$$E_d(idle) = Pwd(idle)T_G \left(1 - \sum_{i \in sw} \frac{C_i + C_{sw}}{P_i}\right)$$

//$P_{wd}(idle)$: average processor idle power   [7.10]

$$E_d(hw) = T_G \sum_{i \in hw} P_{wd}(i) \frac{C_i}{P_i}$$ [7.11]

For flexibility and genericity concerns, the task average dynamic power values $P_{wd}(i)$ are normalized versus the supply voltage and clock frequency and the average task static power is expressed by area unit (W/gate or W/µm² as indicated in [ITR 03]).

7.5.2.5. Static power/energy metric

The available static power, usually given by means of mW/area, depends mainly of the leakage power, the supply voltage, the transistor count and a technology-dependent parameter:

$$Pw_s = f(N_{tr} K_{design} I_{leakage} V_{dd})$$ [7.12]

Our model uses $Pw_s(sw)$ and $Pw_s(hw)$ for software and hardware parts respectively. A dynamic strategy can be adopted for static power management if hardware accelerator power supply can be switched off when unused. In such a case the average static power dissipation is given by:

$$Pw_s = Pw_{offsw} \times Area(sw) + Pw_{offhw} \times \sum_{i \in hw} Area(i) \frac{C_i}{P_i}$$ [7.13]

Without HW dynamic power supply management, we obtain:

$$Pw_s = Pw_{offsw} \times Area(sw) + Pw_{offhw} \times \sum_{i \in hw} Area(i) \qquad [7.14]$$

7.5.2.6. *Partitioning Algorithm*

7.5.2.6.1. Solution evaluation

The main difficulties during the partitioning/RT scheduling algorithm are firstly the size of the design space, especially since multiple granularity solutions can be considered for each hardware task implementation, and secondly the iterative scheduling of task worst case response time.

```
Boolean Schedulable (S){
        U = ProcUseRate(S) // Processor use rate
        IF (U+rs > 1) // rs: server task CPU ratio
                RETURN false;

        ELSE IF  U + rs ≤ n*(2^(1/n) − 1)  RETURN true;
        ELSE {
                FOR ALL T_i by Increasing Priority Order
                        R_i = ExactResponseTimeAnalysis(Ti);
                        IF R_i > P_i RETURN false;
                RETURN true;
        }
}
```

Figure 7.5. *Schedulability test*

A solution is valid if firstly all tasks meet their deadlines and secondly if the current cost belongs to the N first best costs. Contrary to the response time computation, the cost is not iterative and must be evaluated first. Thus, the schedulability is computed in a three-step approach (see Figure 7.5) in order to restrict the use of iterative response time computations. The algorithm first tests if the processor rate is lower than 1. As a second test, the fast rate monotonic analysis (RMA) is performed, it gives a sufficient but not necessary condition for schedulability. Finally, if the first tests are valid, an exact analysis is performed. Note that the designer can specify the CPU ratio *rs* to be guaranteed for the server task.

7.5.2.6.2. Design space exploration

Two methods are currently available: the first one is exact and based on the Branch & Bound (B&B) algorithm, while the second one is heuristic and uses a simulated Annealing approach (SA). The B&B starts with a left edge branch representing a complete software solution and progresses towards a complete hardware. Schedulability tests solutions with the finest granularity degree. Tasks are ranked in a branch according to the priority order. On a given branch, for each task added, the cost is first evaluated; if the cost is lower than the best current solution, then the task schedulability is computed according to the method described in Figure 7.5. When the cost is larger than the best value or when the solution is not schedulable then a new task implementation is evaluated. If no more implementation is available, another implementation is considered for the previous task in the current branch and so on. The main difficulty occurs when a hardware solution with a fine granularity implies the insertion of a communication task with a shorter period than its predecessor in the branch. In such a case, the schedulability of previous tasks with a lower priority must be computed again. The B&B is efficient even for large graphs (100 tasks) when there are few schedulable solutions, but its computation is prohibitive when numerous solutions are proposed for each task. When the response time computation dramatically slows down the design space exploration, the SA heuristic can efficiently relay the B&B.

7.6. UMTS FDD Case Study

The A3S profile has been created to specify the software defined radio physical layer in the UML 2.0 meta-model. A UMTS FDD channel in uplink mode has been chosen as a first reference to determine which software and hardware components could be included in the software and hardware components library from the A3S UML profile. This application has also been tested to validate the A3S tool. The UMTS transmitter and receiver applications have been modeled through two different activity diagrams (UMTS receiver modeled in Figure 7.2). The chosen hardware platform corresponds to a standard board composed of multiple DSPs connected to FPGAs via FIFO and SDRAM memories. The deployment diagram represents this Pentek board (4292) described thanks to the hardware components from the A3S hardware components library (an overview is given on Figure 7.3). For this case study the partitioning has been determined manually by the designer. After having specified the hardware components attributes using the Pentek board components characteristics, and the software components attributes using software IP core characteristics, the validation step and the schedulability performance analysis are performed.

Non-functional attributes are first checked to verify the system coherency. Then the A3S tool generates the GTG file (.gtg) and provides the HW architecture characteristics to perform the schedulability and the power consumption analysis. Our real-time analysis tool has been first designed for mono-processor architectures with hardware accelerators, it has been modified to support schedulability analysis in the context of multi-DSP/Processor architectures.

To prototype the UMTS FDD transmitter and receiver we have considered a hardware platform composed of four TMS320 C6203 DSP running at 300Mhz. Each DSP is connected to a XILINX Virtex XC2V3000 FPGA running at 100Mhz. Each DSP is also connected to an external shared SDRAM memory. The two UMTS FDD software applications, transmitter (SW 1) and receiver (SW 2) are implemented into the hardware platform described above. SW 1 is composed of 11 functions (pulse shaping, scrambling, coding, spreading, integrating, etc.) and SW 2 is composed of 14 functions (matched_filter, rake, descrambling, despreading, decoding, etc.).

	Data rate			Data rate		
	117 kbits/s			950 kbits/s		
	DSP_A	DSP_C	Time (ms)	DSP_A	DSP_C	Time (ms)
Transmitter (SW1)						
1st experience (DSPs)	96.6%	3.4%	9.99	96.6%	5.1%	10.33
2nd experience (DSP + FPGA)	11.4%	3.4%	7.96	11.4%	5.1%	8.26
Receiver (SW2)						
1st experience (DSPs)	185.5%	4.6%	19.27	185.5%	5.0%	19.33
2nd experience (DSP + FPGA)	17.1%	4.6%	9.44	17.2%	5.0%	9.49

Table 7.1. *Hardware component utilization rate*

Different implementations are considered to verify and validate the efficiency of the A3S tool. The first experience consists of implementing all the functions for SW 1 and SW 2 into the DSPs (software solution), and then in modifying the data rate frequency to see the limits of such a solution. The second experience consists of partitioning the functions implementation between DSPs (DSP_A, DSP_C) and their respective associated FPGAs (FPGA_A, FPGA_C). The critical functions within each application are implemented into the FPGAs and the remainder into the DSPs. For both experiences, the two different data rates (117 kbits/s and 950 kbits/s) are tested. The UMTS design under consideration is not a complete fully realistic UMTS system but comprise enough processing element to evaluate the tool.

For each experience, a possible scheduling was determined and the corresponding hardware components utilization rates were computed. The results for one radio frame are given in Table 7.1. An overall 100% means that all the processing power of all HW devices is necessary to run the application in real time. Less than 100% means that real-time is also reached. When the workload is more than 100% it means that a single HW device (DSP or FPGA) is not enough to run the application.

In the UMTS standard, a radio frame must be computed every 10 ms. In this first experience, we only consider the execution time issue. It shows that software-only solution is adequate for SW 1 as the rate is correct (<100%) for the two configurations (117 kbits/950 kbits). Actually this solution is not correct for the 950 kbits configuration since the timing constraint is not respected as the execution time exceeds 10 ms (10.33>10). In the case of SW 2, the software-only solution cannot be realized because of the DSP overload (185%). Thus, to respect both the DSP load and the timing constraint, we have to define a new implementation.

The result analysis helps to identify function and/or data exchanges that affect the global system performance. Changing the implementation is straightforward with the A3S tool since it just requires to modify some links (corresponding to the critical functions) and not to rebuild the whole system. Thus, only two critical functions (PSH for SW1, MFL for SW2) that were previously implemented onto the DSPs are implemented onto the FPGAs (hardware solution corresponding to the 2nd experience). The remainder functions are still implemented onto the same DSPs. The new results show that for each case (SW 1, SW 2), the DSP load was reduced (e.g. from 96% to 11% for SW 1 and from 185% to 17% for SW 2). This implementation also reduces the execution time, and the timing constraint (<10ms) is respected in each case. Thanks to the tool, the designer performs a fast analysis and is able to compare the most appropriate implementations satisfying the application and architecture constraints.

7.7. Conclusion

In this chapter we have presented the UML compliant rapid prototyping A3S tool based on a UML A3S profile. The UML A3S framework provides designers with a unified, fast and easy method to specify software applications and hardware architectures. Such an approach significantly decreases the prototyping time and enhances system reuse, which is a major metric for software radio applications. It also provides to the designer an exploration tool for rapidly testing various HW/SW mappings and performing the corresponding schedulability analysis. Furthermore, the A3S project proposes more than a design framework. It also provides a design methodology to validate complex systems with a step by step design approach from PIM to PSM. This CAD tool simplifies designers job by making automatic usually heavy tasks, like coherency verifications, period task and timing computations as well as scheduling analysis and verification.

7.8. Acknowledgements

This research was sponsored by French National Research and Innovation Program for Telecommunication within the framework of A3S project. We particularly thank Jean-Etienne Goubard from Thales, Nicolas Bulteau and Philippe Desfray from Softeam, and Mickaël Raulet from Mitsubishi Electric ITE-TCL.

7.9. References

[ARA 99] ARAKI D., ISHII T., GAJSKI D. D., *Rapid prototyping with HW/SW codesign tool*, Proceedings. Engineering of Computer-Based Systems (ECBS), pp. 114-121, 1999.

[AZZ 02] AZZEDINE A., DIGUET J-P., PHILIPPE J-L., *Large exploration for HW/SW partitioning of multirate and aperiodic real-time systems*, in 10th Int. Symp. on HW/SW Codesign, Estes Park, USA, 2002.

[BOL 97] BOLSEN I., DE MAN H., LIN B., VAN ROMPAEY K., VERCAUTEREN S., VERKEST D., *Hardware/software co-design of digital telecommunication systems*, Proceedings of IEEE, vol. 85, no. 3, pp. 391-418, 1997.

[BUT 00] BUTTS J.A., SOHI G., *A static power model for architects*, in: 33rd ACM/IEEE Int. Symp. on Microarchitecture, 2000.

[CAL 90] CALVEZ J-P., *MCSE : Spécification et conception des systèmes : une méthodologie*, Masson, 1990.

[DAR 03] Team DaRT 2003, *Dataparallelism for Real-Time*, Activity Report, http://www.inria.fr/rapportsactivite/RA2003/dart2003/dart_tf.html, 2003.

[DAS 99] DASDAN A., *Timing Analysis of Embedded Real-Time Systems*, Ph.D. dissertation, University of Illinois, 1999.

[DAV 01] DAVIS J., HYLANDS C., KIENHUIS B., LEE E.A., LIU J., LIU X., MULIADIS L., NEUENDORFFER S., TSAY J., VOGEL B., XIONG Y., *Ptolemy II: Heterogeneous Concurrent Modeling and Design in Java*, Technical Memorandum, UCB/ERL M01/12, EECS, University of California, Berkeley, CA 94720, March, 2001.

[DAV 98] DAVE P., JHA N.K., *Casper: Concurrent hardware-software co-synthesis of hard real-time aperiodic specification of embedded system architectures*, in: Design, Automation & Test in Europe Conf., Paris, France, 1998.

[EDW 97] EDWARDS S. A., LAVAGNO L., LEE E. A., SANGIOVANNI-VINCENTELLI A., *Design of Embedded Systems: Formal Models, Validation and Synthesis*, Proceedings of IEEE, Vol. 85,N°3, pp. 366-390, 1997.

[ERN 93] ERNST R., HENKEL J., BENNER T., *Hardware-Software Cosynthesis for Microcontrollers*, IEEE Journal Design and Test of Computers, pp. 64-75, 1993.

[FRO 04] FROHLICH D., BEIERLEIN T., STEINBACH B., *Object-Oriented Co-Design for Run-Time Reconfigurable Architectures with UML™*, 5th International Conference on Computer Aided Design of Discrete Devices (CAD DD'04), 2004.

[GAJ 04] GAJSKI D. D., *System-Level Design Methodology*, ASP-DAC 2004 Pacifico Yokohama, Yokohama, Japan, January 27, 2004.

[GUP 93] GUPTA R., DE MICHELI G., *Hardware-Software Cosynthesis for Digital Systems*, IEEE Design and Test of Computers, pp. 29-41, 1993.

[ITR 03] S. I. Association, *International technology roadmap for semiconductors*, http://public.itrs.net/Files/2003ITRS/Home2003.htm, 2003.

[JOS 86] JOSEPH M., PANDYA P., *Finding response time in a real-time system*, IEEE Design and Test of Computers 29 (5) 390-395, 1986.

[LAV 02] LAVAGNO L., MARTIN G., SELIC B.V., *UML for Real : Design of Embedded Real-Time Systems*, Kluwer Academic Publishers, 2002.

[MIT 95] MITOLA J., *The Software Radio Architecture*, IEEE Communications Magazine, vol.. 33, no. 5, pp. 26-38, 1995.

[OBJ 06] Objecteering Software, http://www.objecteering.com/

[QFP 05] *UML profile for QoS and Fault Tolerance Characteristics and Mechanisms*, (http://www.omg.org/docs/ptc/05-05-02.pdf) , May 2005.

[SDR 06] SOFTWARE DESIGN RADIO FORUM, http://www.sdrforum.org

[SHU 03] SHULAS. S. K., TALPIN J-P., EDWARDS S. A., GUPTA R. K., *High Level Modeling and Validation Methodologies for Embedded Systems: Bridging the Productivity Gap*, 16th International Conference on VLSI design, pp. 9-14, 2003.

[SPP 03] *UML profile for Schedulability, Performance and Time Specification*, (http://www.omg.org/docs/formal/03-09-01.pdf) , September 2003.

[SRP 05] *UML profile for Software Radio*, (http://www.omg.org/docs/dtc/05-09-05.pdf), May 2005.

[SYS 03] SysML Object Management Group, *UML for System Engineering Request for Proposal*, 2003.

[TMA 04] TMAR H., DIGUET J-P., AZZEDINE A., ABID M., PHILIPPE J-L., *RTDT: a Static QoS Manager, RT Scheduling, HW/SW Partitioning CAD Tool*, ICM, 2004.

CHAPTER 8

Model Driven Testing
of Time Sensitive Distributed Systems

Chapter written by Borislav Gajanovic, Hans Grönniger and Bernhard Rumpe

Software Systems Engineering
Technische Universität Braunschweig
Braunschweig, Germany
www.sse.cs.tu-bs.de
b.gajanovic@sse.cs.tu-bs.de,{h.groenniger,b.rumpe}@tu-bs.de

8.1. Model Driven Testing

Software engineering in recent years has come up with a larger portfolio of techniques and methods to measure and improve or ensure quality of software products. Among those methods we have available inspection and review techniques for all artifacts that are produced during development. These techniques require clear quality criteria as well as an appropriate process that clarifies the order of artifacts to be delivered and examined.

Among the most promising techniques today, however, is the execution of "running" versions of system descriptions and the check of the execution result against the desired result. Agile methods [BEC 99a, COC 02, BEC 01, RUM 04] have furthermore successfully demonstrated that a full automation of the testing process is of high value in any larger and quality driven project. Only automated tests can efficiently be reused by developers.

The portfolio of testing techniques has become large. It ranges from functional tests on abstract specifications over black box tests, stress tests, random tests down to glass box tests derived from the code. As testing has become a powerful technique, it was a natural idea to lift the use of testing techniques from the late coding phase to earlier phases, where fixing errors is less costly. However, starting early with testing means, we need executable artifacts early in the development process. If requirement specifications or at least design and architectural artifacts are executable, they need to (a) be defined precisely and (b) describe not only structural aspects but also behavioral issues. This calls for precisely defined modeling languages and for tools dealing with those languages. Tools need to be able to analyze well-formedness (thus checking context conditions) and to animate the model or to be able to map the model to code.

The necessary properties of a model strongly depend on the context of the model usage. Models can be used for constructive or for test code generation. The desired properties here are fundamentally different. In case of a constructive code generation, we do have a compiler and as "side effect" modeling is equal to implementation. We can reuse the generated code as implementation if it is compatible not only with the development computers, but also with the target and is efficient enough. Instead, if we want to generate testing code, we do neither need complete and therefore very detailed models, nor do we need to restrict us to an executable modeling language. To understand the difference, consider a post condition for a method of the form $a^n = b^n + c^n$ Æ a, b, c, n > 2. Conditions like that are very easy to check, but it is usually extremely hard to construct a program that finds such values. So the choice of appropriate modeling languages and styles during the various development stages is important.

Statecharts [HAR 87] are among the most interesting forms of descriptions for executable behavior. The use of underspecified Statecharts [PAE 94, KLE 97] with transition conditions and actions in (almost) first-order-logic makes it possible to generate checking code only, but not constructive code. A clever choice of appropriate modeling techniques and their underlying semantics is therefore inevitable.

For early checking of requirements, it is necessary to have a concise modeling technique and an efficient way of simulating the models at hand. In this chapter we demonstrate an approach used to early validate requirements on distributed systems. This approach is exemplary, but demonstrates what can be achieved when using:

- concise, compact modeling techniques in early phases,

- tools for transforming modeling techniques to executable languages,

- a lean process to develop and use the models during the development adequately.

To demonstrate the approach, we choose a relatively simple, but not too simplistic protocol, namely the Alternating Bit Protocol (ABP) [BRO 01]. The two modeling languages used for structure and behavior are adapted versions of UML diagrams: the composite structure diagrams and (flat) Statecharts respectively state machines. As the protocol is useful for distributed asynchronously communication systems, we choose the use of streams as underlying technical domain, because it offers very precise semantics as well as a good integration of composition, refinement and various styles of specification [BRO 01, RUM 97]. For a lean development, we use a Haskell [THO 99, BIR 98] interpreter to simulate the models. For example, Haskell provides lazy evaluation of lists, which makes it possible to almost perfectly simulating streams as potentially infinite observations over communication channels.

The remainder of this paper introduces the concept of distributed systems (section 8.2), the Alternating Bit Protocol (section 8.3), the general approach on testing (section 8.4) and the application of testing strategies on the ABP (section 8.5). Finally our findings are discussed (section 8.6).

8.2 Asynchronous Communication in Distributed Systems

In this section we briefly introduce the used semantic framework that describes on asynchronous communication as underlying communication principle of our framework. In a distributed system, we do have active components that communicate with each other through asynchronous sending and receiving of messages. We assume communication is based on unidirectional channels. For a precise modeling of their behavior, we use observation histories that describe what happens on these channels over time using the mathematical concept of streams. Streams are thus used to model the message-flow over those channels. The behavior of a component is specified through a description of the input-output relation on these streams.

A stream is a finite or an infinite sequence of messages from some fixed finite set of possible messages (type). A stream-based specification of a component consists of a black box and an arbitrary (but finite) number of directed input and output channels. In Figure 8.1 a composition of a system from several components is shown. With a single stream we describe the history on one channel, a component behavior is given by a function mapping its input streams to output streams. Certain restrictions apply on these functions to ensure the behavior is well-defined, for example, a component (and thus a function) cannot undo messages that have been emitted, and it cannot react on future input (and thus predict the future).

For any realizable component there is a stream-processing function with the same input/output behavior. Any state machine (with possibly infinite number of states) whose state transition function acts on messages appearing at the input and is yielding appropriate streams on the output can also be defined via a stream-processing function [RUM 97, RUM 99]. Together with the fact that semantic definition through stream processing functions support composition of components via channels, we are able to use state machines and a variant of composite structure diagrams as a comprehensive specification language on a well-defined semantic basis. These stream processing functions are the primary concept to be mapped to Haskell for execution and testing. Furthermore, specification languages are particularly powerful if they allow us to abstract from implementation details and provide concepts for underspecification (alternatives, etc.). In terms of our underlying formalism, this means that a specification does not correspond to a single function, but to a set of functions that describes a set of possible implementations.

The list given below describes a basic set of operators on streams useful for the specification of the components. For a comprehensive introduction to the stream-based specification and development technique see [BRO 01].

- $[M]$ - The set of all streams over a set of messages M.

- $[]$ - The symbol for the empty stream.

- $[c]$ - The stream consisting of a message c.

- head s - Yields the first message of a non-empty stream s.

- tail s - Returns the rest of a nonempty stream.

- $\#s$ - Returns the length of a stream s (may be N [{1}).

- s_1 ++ s_2 - The concatenation of s_1 and s_2.

- filter S s - Filtering a stream s with respect to the members of a set S.

Please note the special case $\#s = 1$) s_1 ++ $s_2 = s1$. Also note that some operators like length # count infinite things and therefore cannot be used in an implementation.

As an additional concept, we need the idea of time to model time-sensitive systems. Time can easily be modeled through the introduction of a special "message" - here symbolized with Tk and pronounced as tick - into the underlying set of messages. For that purpose we define an operator T for the introduction of so-called timed streams over a set of messages M:

$$T\ M = \{\ s\ |\ s\ 2\ [M[\ \{Tk\}]\ \ \text{Æ}\ \ \#(\texttt{filter}\ \{Tk\}\ s) = 1$$

A tick in a stream represents the incrementation of a global digital clock in the system. The time is never ending so there are infinitely many ticks in a timed stream. Timed streams are nothing more than normal infinite streams with a special structure. Hence, all operations introduced in the previous section can be applied to the timed streams as well.

8.3 The Alternating Bit Protocol

In this section we describe how to apply our approach to a simple version of the Alternating Bit Protocol that can be found in [BRO 01, BRO 93]. We use the Alternating Bit Protocol here as a simple example of a time sensitive distributed system which transmits data safely over unreliable media. The black box specification of the ABP is simple: abstracting from possible delays, the ABP is the identity. An appropriate specification of the ABP is therefore given through a set of stream processing functions:

$$ABP \propto T\,M!\,T\,M$$

where for any input *inp* 2 T M we have the abstraction of timing information on input and resulting output is identical:

$$\texttt{filter}\,M\,(\texttt{ABP}\,inp) = \texttt{filter}\,M\,inp$$

8.3.1. *Informal Description of the ABP Components*

The problem to be solved by the ABP is to transmit information over an unreliable medium. Thus the ABP must be decomposed (in a simplified version) as shown in Figure 8.1. The system consists of a sender, a receiver and two transportation media. Both versions of the media are identical, except for the transported kind of messages. The medium is assumed to be given (e.g. in form of the internet or a bus). This means the model of the medium describes a given situation. In contrast, the sender and the receiver have to be defined in such a way that the overall specification is correct. Our task is therefore to model all four components accordingly.

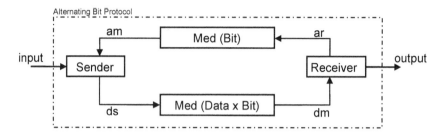

Figure 8.1. *The alternating bit protocol as a composition of its components*

The medium on the bottom of the figure is used to transport signed data items from the sender to the receiver, whereas the upper medium transports the acknowledgements back to the sender. However, the media occasionally lose or delay messages (see details below). To detect loss of messages, the basic idea is to tag the message by a number and let the receiver acknowledge the tagged message by replying the number. If a message or acknowledgement gets lost, the sender repeats the message after a while (timeout).

We assume there is only one message in transmission: the sender stores forthcoming messages in a buffer until the last sent one is acknowledged. For reasons of efficiency, the message numbering can now be replaced by a single bit that alternates for each message. Thus, each data item from the input channel is alternatingly signed by the sender using a bit. The receiver returns the bit and writes the corresponding data to the output. If a message or an acknowledgement was delayed too long, then the sender resends the message. Details like what happens when the delay is too long can be deduced from the below given specification. To model an unreliable, but not demonic transportation medium, we assume the medium to have the following properties:

1. If a message is sent infinitely often, then it will pass infinitely often;

2. The medium does not change the order in which the messages have been sent;

3. The medium does not duplicate messages or alters the message content.

Number 1) is a typical fairness condition on a medium. In other words it is always possible to transmit an item through an unreliable medium within some finite (but unknown) number of transmission attempts. In the following section we give a formal, stream-based specification of the above system.

8.3.2. *Stream-Based Specification*

The structure of the complete system is already given through the composition of its components in Figure 8.1. This diagram is a variant of UML's composite structure diagrams that allows us to specify a complete system by the composition of its components (resp. "parts"), the components communicating asynchronously via unidirectional channels as described in section 8.2. In the reminder of this section we can therefore concentrate on the specification of each individual component. We use state machines to model the component's behavior. Since we enable a potentially infinite number of states, we graphically partition the state space into equivalence classes. These classes are given as invariants over variables inside the (graphically visible) states. To precisely represent the state space, we define the data types of these variables in form of a box (similar to a class definition in class diagrams). Transitions are of the form {pre} i /o1,..,on {post} where pre and post denote the transition pre- and post-condition, i represents the input and o1,..,on is a sequence of outputs.

Sender: The sender is a time sensitive, "intelligent" component of the protocol. In fact it is the most complicated component in the system. We specify the main functionality of the sender given above through the following state machine.

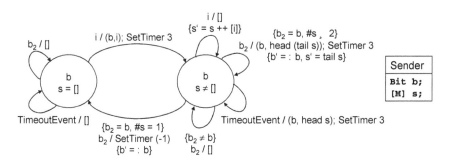

Figure 8.2. *State machine for the sender component*

The sender component owns two input channels: the data input channel (*input*) and the acknowledgement channel (*am*). For reasons of readability, we do not add the channel names to the inputs. Although we do have two input channels, we can distinguish inputs from the channels, as their types are disjoint (Boolean vs. abstract type Message). For an understanding of the specified behavior, the reader may assume that we conceptually "merge" the two input streams in order to be able to let the state machine fire on the union of incoming events from both channels. The sender's state space basically contains the unbounded buffer for data items still to be sent, and by the expected acknowledgement bit. The handling of time is assumed to be done by a timer that "controls" the state machine by filtering SetTimer-events from its output and injecting TimeoutEvent to its input. So, formally, input and output of the state machine (but not the sender itself) are extended by TimeoutEvent resp. SetTimer-messages.

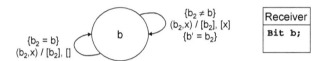

Figure 8.3. *State machine for the medium component*

Medium: For specification of unreliable media in the described form either set based specifications or oracles are used. The unreliability of the medium is a given property which cannot be overcome, but needs to be modeled. Therefore, we handle oracles for both media as two inherent system parameters. An oracle is an infinite binary stream which predicts the behavior of a particular medium over a complete communication history. As the media are time-insensitive components, there is no need to consider time in the corresponding specifications. Instead, this is done systematically (and then automatically when mapped to code) through a simple time extension of the transition-function of a corresponding state machine. This extension just ignores incoming time events. The following state machine specifies untimed polymorphic media with the above properties. However, an additional predicate #(filter {1} o) = 1 is needed to describe the desired fairness property as an assumption on any oracle o.

Receiver: Just like the media, the receiver is also a time insensitive component and can straightforwardly be specified as shown in the following figure.

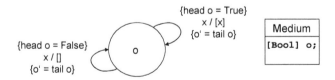

Figure 8.4. *State machine for the receiver component*

8.3.3. *A Mapping to Haskell*

To be able to run tests based on the above given specification, we need a compiler or interpreter that resembles the underlying communication primitives appropriately. We choose the functional language Haskell, for a number of reasons. Most importantly, the Haskell type of lists can be directly taken to represent streams. Therefore, we will now show how to automatically transform the system specified above into an executable Haskell [THO 99, BIR 98, JON 03, HUD 99] program. First we need appropriate data types. We introduce the type Bit to represent the corresponding type in the specification. Then the type constructor Ticked is introduced to inject the time in streams as described in the previous section. A timed stream of as is abbreviated with T a. Oracles are represented as streams of Boolean values. The type of a state machine's delta function is aliased with DeltaFct s i o where s is the state, i the input and o the output type. As the concept of union of sets is not directly present in Haskell, we use the type constructor MergeAB a b to represent the union of two types a and b. The rest of data type definitions allow the addition of a timeout event or the setting of a timer value to a given type a.

```
type Bit = Bool
data Ticked a = V a | Tk
type T a = [Ticked a]
type Oracle = [Bool]
type DeltaFct s i o = (s -> i -> (s,[o]))
data MergeAB a b   = A a | B b
data TimerOut a    = MsgO a | SetTimer Int
data TimerIn a     = MsgI a | TimeoutEvent
```

Runtime system: To keep the generated "code" as simple as possible, to facilitate reuse and to avoid generation of the same functions over and over again, the code is generated against a runtime system. This is quite common, as usually some concepts of the source domain need to be simulated in the target domain. Due to space constraints, only the type definitions of functions we use are shown here. First, we use a function to execute state machines. execSTM takes a state, a delta function and a list of inputs and produces a list of corresponding outputs. execSTM works on timed transition functions as well as untimed ones. To inject time (for time-insensitive descriptions) the timedDelta function is used. It basically adds behavior that resembles a loop transition to every state, consuming a Tick at the input and emitting a Tick at the output. The mergeAB function merges two streams, thus covering the merge of messages from several inputs, while retaining the source channel in the constructors name (see merge type above). The sender contains transitions that control a timer. In fact, we're able to use timers in a state machine. The

addTimer function takes a delta function containing these timer control state-
ments and generates a timed delta function that reacts to the corresponding
events. Please recall that the timed function using ticks to model time is the
final goal.

```
execSTM     :: s -> DeltaFct s i o -> ([i] -> [o])
timedDelta :: DeltaFct s i o -> DeltaFct s (Ticked i) (Ticked o)
mergeAB     :: T a -> T b -> T (MergeAB a b)
addTimer    :: DeltaFct s (TimerIn i) (TimerOut o) ->
                              DeltaFct (s,Int) (Ticked i) (Ticked o)
```

Sender: We use the sender component to demonstrate the mapping of a state machine to Haskell that interacts with our runtime system, because it has an untimed
specification, but uses a timer to check timeouts.

The SenderState consists of the last sent bit and the unbounded message buffer.
The input to the sender SenderIn is either a message of type a, the acknowledgement
bit or some timeout event (generated by the internal timer). SenderOut defines the
sender output as an alternating bit together with a message of type a but may also be
a setting of a timer. The function senderDelta now basically is a one-to-one mapping
from the specification (see Figure 8.2). We use pattern matching on the current state
and input to define the delta function. Note that transitions with the same inputs and
states but with different pre-conditions are handled in an if-then-else statement.
Timer functionality is added to the sender's delta function using addTimer, giving
the new delta function Delta's.

According to Figure 8.1 the sender takes an input stream and a stream of acknowledgements am and emits a stream of messages with an alternating bit. We
have chosen to merge the input and the bit stream (in accordance with the specification). To complete the mapping, the sender state machine is executed on this merged
stream, starting with the alternating bit set to True, an empty buffer and disabled
timer (-1).

```
type SenderState a = (Bit,[a])
type SenderIn   a = TimerIn (MergeAB a Bit)
type SenderOut  a = [TimerOut (Bit,a)]


senderDelta:: SenderState a -> SenderIn a ->(SenderState a,SenderOut a)
senderDelta (b,   []) (MsgI (A i)) = ((b,[i]),[MsgO(b,i), SetTimer 3])
senderDelta (b,   xs) (MsgI (A i)) = ((b,xs++[i]),[])
senderDelta (b,   []) (MsgI (B b2)) = ((b,[]),[])
```

```
senderDelta (b, x:xs) (MsgI (B b2)) =
      if      b/=b2   then ((b,x:xs),    [])
      else if null xs then ((not b,[] ), [SetTimer (-1)])
      else ((not b,xs),   [MsgO (not b,head(xs)),SetTimer 3])
senderDelta (b,[])   TimeoutEvent = ((b,[]),[])
senderDelta (b,x:xs) TimeoutEvent = ((b,x:xs), [MsgO (b,x),SetTimer 3])
sDelta' = addTimer senderDelta


sender :: T a -> T Bit -> T (Bit,a)
sender is am = (execSTM ((True,[]),-1) sDelta') (mergeAB is am)
```

For the **Medium** and **Receiver** component, only the type definitions are shown. They also correspond to the respective state machine specification and therefore illustrate that the resulting system will be composed. Please note that the receiver component has to start with the same acknowledgement bit True as the sender (see above).

```
mediumDelta :: Oracle -> a -> (Oracle,[a])
medium :: Oracle -> T a -> T a

receiverDelta :: Bit -> (Bit,a) -> (Bit, [Bit],[a] )
receiver :: T (Bit,a) -> (T Bit,T a)
```

8.3.4. *Executing the Model*

Finally the complete system is just a composition of its components (compare Figure 8.1). Since we have a feedback loop in the system, we need to insert a start-up delay. This delay is inserted as an extra Tick prepended to the second medium's output.

```
abp :: (Oracle,Oracle) -> T a -> T a
abp (os1,os2) is - out
   where (as,out) = receiver dm
         dm       = medium os1 ds
         am       = Tk:(medium os2 as) -- delay for feedback
         ds       = sender is am
```

8.4. Strategies for Testing Distributed, Asynchronously Communicating Systems

Based on the model of our system and our mapping of the model to Haskell we can now discuss strategies for testing distributed, asynchronously communicating systems. After some general comments on testing, we discuss how to systematically derive test cases from our component models as well as from the composition model. Then we demonstrate how these test cases can be implemented in (or generated for) Haskell in a lightweight manner, i.e. not depending on any complex third-party test framework, but exploiting the special features of higher-order functional programming languages. First, we recall some general rules for developers and testers [MYE 79] that also apply for testing of models:

1. The tests should be regression-enabled. That means that if the program changes, the test can be replayed easily to check if all tested properties still hold. How this is supported by a lightweight test infrastructure is mainly described in section 8.5.

2. The tests should be kept local. This is a general problem of complex software where it is often the case that testing some method of an object means also executing many other interlocked methods of other objects with possible side-effects. Object oriented systems do provide their own solutions through substituting parts of the context through stubs.

    Keeping test cases focused also applies to functional programs, where this kind of substitution through subclassing unfortunately does not exist. In the context of Haskell, we examine techniques that help programmers to write effective test cases for the generated functions.

3. The quality of the test cases should be assessed. A wide range of techniques exists to assess the quality of the tests. Since we use state machines for component specification, well known coverage criteria like transition coverage, etc. can be applied directly [BIN 99].

8.4.1. *Rules for Testing of Distributed Functionally Specified Models*

Testing models for distributed, asynchronously communicating programs implemented in Haskell as we did, in principle, means testing functions.

In general we can benefit from the fact that these functions are side-effect free. That means we can concentrate on the input and output behavior of the function under test for black-box testing (and the structure of the function, for glass-box testing). Regardless of the type of system we construct, there are some generally applicable rules that ease the testing of functional programs. For example, the rules from equivalence class testing [BIN 99] can be applied. Basically that means that by looking at the function as a black-box and an informal specification one can identify input values that are treated uniformly by the function and make these an equivalence class. From each equivalence class it is regarded as sufficient to select one value and test this as a representative for the respective class. Furthermore, corner cases or extreme values like empty lists, empty strings, number zero and so on should be tested as well. It's also advisable to keep functions simple and avoid embedded lambda abstractions because anonymous functions are not (easily) testable. Functional programs usually are defined using rules with pattern matching. Coverage of these rules as well as their input patterns is also advisable.

As we do not in general deal with testing of functional programs, but with a special kind of programs generated from our state machine-based models, we now concentrate on the state machine-based testing approach, although we will discover that the principles discussed so far lead to very similar test cases. As said earlier, well-known test strategies for state machines do exist and can be reused.

As we described in section 8.3.3, our system includes a "runtime" part. Here we provide standard functions for example to execute state machines, to add a notion of time and to handle timers as addendum to state machines. Since this functionality remains the same regardless of the individual system and since we generate code against this functionality in a systematic way, we are able to ignore the runtime system for test case generation and concentrate on the specific part which resembles mainly the untimed state transition (delta) functions for the individual components. This leads to a more comprehensible and optimized set of test cases for each component. However, we also keep in mind that we need to make system tests that check the functionality of the overall ABP component.

For each component's delta function the test cases should fulfil transition coverage. That means every transition is executed at least once. Since we allow pre- and post-conditions in transitions, every expression in a disjunction is evaluated to True at least once. Note that this kind of decision coverage is not relevant for the ABP example as there are no disjunctions. In general disjunctions in these conditions should (and often can) be transformed by splitting the transition and handling the resulting transitions separately. If every state is reachable, transition coverage on state machines subsumes state coverage. However, we have to distinguish the finitely many states of the graphically depicted state machine and the potentially infinite number of states (and transitions) of the implementation. The relationship between both is handled by grouping the state space into equivalence classes using invariants. However, transition coverage now does not imply coverage of these equivalence classes anymore. Thus coverage criteria for state equivalence classes and transitions can be combined.

Beyond transition coverage, it is interesting to check the combined behavior of transitions, e.g. using full paths through the state machine. A minimized path coverage might check every path, where loops are only handled once (similar to "boundary-interior path tests" [NTA 88]). This technique is costly, as paths may be many, but also helpful, because some errors only occur in the combination of unusual paths, which nobody has considered.

As a last issue to be considered, the input itself may be analyzed to derive possible tests. As we deal with streams of incoming messages, equivalence classes of messages may be considered, but also sequences of messages (e.g. what happens if the same message arrives twice?) or certain interleavings. This may lead to further refinements of the test cases. However, as variants of messages are usually handled through different pattern of inputs, coverage on input messages may be implied by coverage on transitions.

8.5. Implementing Tests in Haskell

Having clarified general considerations, we now show how to define test cases in a systematic way and show how they can be executed in an efficient manner, to allow us to perform regression testing.

8.5.1. *Test Infrastructure*

Only a few generic functions are needed that serve as the test infrastructure similar to the runtime system discussed above. These functions later allow us to write test cases concisely, similarly to unit test frameworks for other languages (e.g. [BEC 99b]). At first, we introduce a transition tester. transT takes the input and current state, executes a transition and compares the result with the expected state and output.

```
transT:: DeltaFct s i o -> (s, i , s,[o]) -> Bool
transT delta (s,i,expS,expO) = ((delta s i) == (expS, expO))
```

Second, we introduce a path tester. The full path tester pathT checks whether a sequence of inputs leads to a certain path of states and sequence of outputs. Slightly adapted versions of a path tester just check the state or the output. It is up to the test engineer to decide how fine granular a test needs to be defined. All versions take a transition function, a start state and a sequence of inputs. The implementation is straightforward and omitted here since we are not going to give concrete examples for path tests in this chapter. Non-deterministic transition functions are realized through an oracle, which allows us to fully control non-determinism, but forces us to cover different oracles as well (not shown in the signatures below).

```
pathT  :: DeltaFct s i o -> (s, [i], [s,[o]]) -> [Bool]
pathTs :: DeltaFct s i o -> (s, [i], [s]) -> Bool
pathTo :: DeltaFct s i o -> (s, [i], [o]) -> Bool
```

8.5.2. *Tests for the ABP Components*

We will now illustrate the implementation of test cases in Haskell considering the sender component as an example. Our goal is to manually derive transition coverage for the sender and show how these transitions can be denoted easily. The sender component has a total of eight transitions that need to be tested. This leads to eight tests to cover the state machine transitions.

We start by explaining how a test case that covers a single transition can be derived from the state machine specification. As an example, consider the following transition from Figure 8.2:

```
{b2 = b, #s , 2}
  b2 / (b, head (tail s)); SetTimer 3
{b' = :b, s' = tail s}
```

Furthermore, the transition's source and destination state is characterized by a non-empty buffer. First, we need to identify a valid start state for the transition. Since the buffer needs to be non-empty and, due to the pre-condition, at least two messages long, one possible start state can be (True, [3,4]). The transition's input is a bit b2 whose value is restricted by the pre-condition. To test the specification, we derive the appropriate resulting state and output not from the model, but determine from our background knowledge what must happen. In this setting it is necessary to act as test oracle ourselves, as we are going to check the specification. We merely analyze the transition system to understand, what transitions need to be covered. In this case, we derive the resulting state (False, [4]) and expected output [(False,4),SetTimer 3]. The rest of the sender transitions can be handled in the same manner. A further detailing is not necessary, because neither an oracle nor internal complicated pre/postconditions occur, nor is the sender incompletely specified. We collect all transition tests in a table below.

Please note that as in the defining state transition diagram, we do not need to tag the incoming input, because the values on both channels are disjoint. Boolean values are acknowledgements and integers are used as messages. As discussed, the corresponding Haskell definitions need to deal with this union of channels, resulting in a more awkward and less readable definition. Let us assume they are given in a list called senderTransitionTests. The defined transition tests can systematically be mapped to Haskell. Together with the earlier mentioned functions (and possible path tests for the sender) a test suite is defined easily:

no.	source state	input	destination state	output
1	(True,[])	True	(True,[])	[]
2	(True,[])	3	(True,[3])	[(True,3),SetTimer 3]
3	(True,[3])	4	(True,[3,4])	[]
4	(True,[3,4])	True	(False,[4])	[(False,3),SetTimer 3]
5	(True,[4])	True	(False,[])	[SetTimer (-1)]
6	(True,[3,4])	False	(True,[3,4])	[]
7	(True,[3,4])	TimeoutEvent	(True,[3,4])	[(True,3),SetTimer 3]
8	(True,[])	TimeoutEvent	(True,[])	[]

```
senderTestSuite = map (transT senderDelta) senderTransitionTests
```

To execute the sender test we consequently only need to evaluate senderT-estSuite, receiving a larger list of Booleans (hopefully all True. Using the definition

```
all = and (senderTestSuite ++ receiverTestSuite ++ ...)
```

allows us to resemble the well known "green/red"-light from unit testing. Due to space limitations, only the test case definition and execution for the sender component is shown. Analogously, component tests for the medium and receiver can be derived. However, the media exhibit special characteristics that we have not dealt with so far, as they use an oracle. As we can understand the oracle as a special case of input sequence, we therefore just need to analyze possible interesting inputs sequences and run those together with the other tests.

We showed how to systematically define and execute test cases for delta functions of state machines. Especially for system level testing of the composed ABP function it might also be useful to generate a larger set of test cases randomly. Since this is not in the focus of this chapter we refer the reader for example to [CLA 00, KOO 03].

8.6. Discussion of Results

In this chapter, we have discussed an approach to model behavior of distributed asynchronously communication behavior. To test these models we had to map them into an executable form. We chose the functional language Haskell for that purpose, because Haskell offers lazy lists as well as pattern matching techniques, which perfectly allow us to simulate our underlying semantics.

As a next step, we have understood how tests cover transitions, state, input or even paths. This allows us to systematically derive tests. However, our approach of an automatic mapping ("code generation") of the model into the simulation engine does not allow us to derive complete tests from the model. Deriving code and tests from the same model does not allow us to check correctness of the model, but consistency of the generators. Thus, our approach so far only allows us to understand what test inputs are of specific interest, but forces us to manually add the desired test result to the test. The situation changes when we do a manual implementation of the model. Then this simulation engine can be used to derive test results that can be used as test oracles for the actual implementation.

When applying this approach to other distributed systems, we found the approach very effective for us developers. Through systematic and early definition of tests, we found some subtle errors very early in the specification model. Deriving tests from requirement and design models is worth the effort – particularly in complex distributed settings and when validating protocols.

8.7. References

[BAL 98]   BALZERT H., Lehrbuch der Software-Technik. Software-Management, Software-Qualitätssicherung, Unternehmensmodellierung, Spektrum Akademischer Verlag. Heidelberg 1998.

[BEC 99a] BECK K., Extreme Programming Explained. Embrace Change, Addison-Wesley, 1999.

[BEC 99b] BECK K., GAMMA E., "JUnit: A Cook's Tour", JavaReport, August 1999.

[BEC 01]   BECK K., "Aim, Fire (Column on the Test-First Approach)", IEEE Software, vol. 18, num. 5, p. 87-89, IEEE, 2001.

[BIN 99]   BINDER R., Testing Object-Oriented Systems: Models, Patterns, and Tools, Object Technology Series, Addison Wesley, 1999.

[BIR 98]   BIRD R., Introduction to Functional Programming using Haskell, Prentice Hall Series in Computer Science, Prentice Hall, second edition, 1998.

[BRO 93]   BROY M., "Functional Specification of Time Sensitive Communication Systems", ACM Transactions on Software Engineering and Methodology 2:1, p. 1-46, 1993.

[BRO 01]   BROY M., STOLEN K., Specification and Development of Interactive Systems. Focus on Streams, Interfaces and Refinement, Springer Verlag Heidelberg, 2001.

[CLA 00]   CLAESSEN K., HUGHES J., "QuickCheck: a lightweight tool for random testing of Haskell programs", ACM SIGPLAN Notices, vol. 35, num 9, p. 268-279, 2000.

[COC 02]   COCKBURN A., Agile Software Development, Addison-Wesley, 2002.

[HAR 87]   HAREL D., "Statecharts: A Visual Formalism for Complex Systems", Science of Computer Programming, vol. 8, p. 231-274, 1987.

[HUD 99]   HUDAK P., PETERSON J., FASEL J., "A Gentle Introduction to Haskell 98", 1999.

[JON 03]   JONES P., AUGUSTSSON L., BURTON D., BOUTEL B., BURTON W., FASEL J., HAMMOND K., HINZE R., HUDAK P., HUGHES J., JOHNSSON T., JONES M., LAUNCHBURY J., MEIJER E., PETERSON J., REID A., RUNCIMAN C., WADLER P. Haskell 98 Language and Libraries: the Revised Report, Cambridge University Press, 2003.

[KLE 97]   KLEIN C., PREHOFER C., RUMPE B., "Feature Specification and Refinement with State Transition Diagrams", DINI P., Ed., Fourth IEEE Workshop on Feature Interactions in Telecommunications Networks and Distributed Systems, IOS-Press, 1997.

[KOO 03]   KOOPMAN P., PLASMEIJER R., "Testing reactive systems with gast", 2003.

[MYE 79]   MEYERS G., The Art of Software Testing, John Wiley & Sons, New York, 1979.

[NTA 88]   NTAFOS S.C., "A Comparison of Some Structural Testing Strategies", IEEE Trans. Softw. Eng., vol 14, num. 6, p. 868-874, IEEE-Press, 1988.

[PAE 94]   PAECH B., RUMPE B., "A new Concept of Refinement used for Behaviour Modelling with Automata", FME '94, Formal Methods Europe, Symposium '94, LNCS 873, Springer-Verlag, Berlin, October, 1994.

[RUM 97]   RUMPE B., "Formale Methodik des Entwurfs verteilter objektorientierter Systeme", Ausgezeichnete Informatikdissertationen 1997, p. 118-134, Teubner Stuttgart, 1997.

[RUM 99]   RUMPE B., KLEIN C., "Automata Describing Object Behaviour", Object-Oriented Behavioral Specifications, p.265-287, Kluwer Academic Publishers, Norwell, Massachusetts, 1999.

[RUM 04]   RUMPE B., Agile Modellierung mit UML. Codegenerierung, Testfälle, Refactoring, Springer Verlag, 2004.

[THO 99]   THOMPSON S., Haskell: The Craft of Functional Programming, Addison-Wesley Longman Publishing Co., Inc., Boston, MA, USA, 1999.

CHAPTER 9

Model Management for Formal Validation

Chapter written by Joël Champeau, Philippe Dhaussy,
François Mekerke and Jean Charles Roger

ENSIETA –DTN
Brest France
{joel.champeau,philippe.dhaussy,merkekfr,rogerje}@ensieta.fr

9.1. Introduction

The context of this work is in the fields of system engineering and the verification embedded software. In the first one, an important issue is to contribute to the control of the concepts used at system level. MDD approach increases our overall understanding of the system, while allowing us to capitalize a part of this expertise. At system level, expertise is required in several domains, for example, in autonomous robotic platforms; it includes the design of the mechanical parts, the choice of electronics, and the development of the software and the design of control laws. These single tasks have their own technical complexity and they take the system team much time, but it is the combination and interaction that make such a project really complex.

Early integration is the key for a successful project, because the more technical options are opened, the more time-consuming choice and integration become. This is why we need to specify constraints as early as possible, in order to be able to decide whether an option fits into the framework or not. For critical embedded systems, the validation of the temporal dynamic behaviour is a non-functional property which is included in the set of constraints. In order to take this constraint into account, we must provide to the system architects, during the first phases of the life cycle, the means of expression, validation and test of the requirements, which are formulated from the needs expressed by the users of the systems.

To guarantee that a system is correct, it is necessary to show that its implementation well corresponds to specifications expressed from starting requirements. That is driven by the establishment of complementary means to verify that factors of testability like, for example, the performance, reliability, the functional and real-time behavior are well model for the system. The associated properties must be respected during the design and the implementation phases. The evaluation of these factors can be carried out by exploitation of models of whole or part of the system. The checking of models ensures that some properties or precise relations between models are respected. For example, we can illustrate with the checking of non-functional properties like performances or the absence of deadlocks in the behavior.

The problem we face is the following: what can we do to have a fair chance to successfully integrate our system with respect to the constraints, especially the temporal ones? We need the ability to handle two types of entities: representations of system elements and specification/design constraints. We also need a way to apply the latter to the former, in order to get a diagnostic. Constraints or properties to validate can be derived from the requirements and the diagnostics provided by the formal analysis tools, in the case of behavior analysis, must be managed by the system modeling framework. The system architect must be able to handle the requirements and the results of analysis of those in specific, comprehensible views by him, independently of the techniques and formal languages implemented.

Our goal is to formalize a system modeling framework which can be used by a validating process based on the use of requirements modeled in a goal of validation. This chapter is organized in two main parts, one for the definition of the modeling framework and one for the validation process based on the use of requirements expressed in observers. These two studies are in progress independently and the integration is planned in the near future.

So, the first part describes the modeling framework based on the formalization of modeling components which encapsulate domain models. The interconnection of these modeling components is especially emphasised to describe the problematic of model synchronization and transformation.

The second part describes the validation process based on the use of observers at requirements level and model checking techniques. The process includes the management of the system contexts which define the execution contexts of the observer.

9.2. System modeling framework

9.2.1. *Separation of concerns*

As MDD emphasizes separation of the concerns, it is possible to consider modeling a system through several models. Each model focuses on a specific concern of the system; it is formalized thanks to a meta-model dedicated to this concern.

This meta-model can be a restriction of a large meta-model such as for example a subset of UML, or an extension of this one for a non-covered field or even a meta-model completely disconnected from UML to cover a precise domain. We thus note that on this MDD approach rests a whole of models formalized by meta-models. Beyond the aspect of transformations, a new need thus appears to express or formalize interconnections of meta-models. This need appears for example within frameworks of modeling system where many points of view contribute to the description of the total system.

We agree with Steimann on the idea that domains are aspect-free (see [St05]), even though the absence of aspects does not mean the absence of analysis needs. This is why we focus on the interfaces between domains, where data must be exchanged and non-functional properties checked.

The work that we describe in this section places in this context of modeling on the system level with models centred on concerns related to the domains which contribute to the realization of an embedded system.

9.2.2. *Domain modeling*

Our approach is based on domain-dedicated modeling. Our definition of a domain is relative to the scope of the project. If we deal with an embedded system, "software" is a domain, on the same level as "hardware", but for software-intensive systems, "software" is the scope, "RTservices" and "networking" being domains. The structuring of our models reflects this domain-centred approach, since we define the concept of **modeling components**. We call this structure "component" because it offers a public part and a private part that is not directly accessible by another component of modeling. In one word, it encapsulates the domain knowledge.

In our laboratory, we work on prototyping hydrographic systems, and the range of domains related to this system development process is wide:

- For the vector: mechanics, fluid mechanics, sensors/actuators, power management, etc;

- For embedded intelligence: control, software, electronics, communication, etc.

Our problem is related to system modeling in general and system integration in particular. In each domain, the work includes the search for available technologies, testing various options, dimensioning a part depending on the others, etc.

These tasks are complex, but we have experts who know how to solve each one of them. The problem stands in the passage from local solutions to global integration. In order to find a global solution, we need to explore the net of dependence relationships between various local solutions. This becomes rapidly difficult, because the size of the design space, i.e. the number of possible configurations, explodes.

9.2.3. *Model Management*

In order to do this, we define **domain models** in which various options can be categorized and stored. Such a model receives all local solutions to the specification in the scope of its domain, first without caring about global integration, then providing only the solutions that comply with additional constraints.

This modeling block is a construct whose purpose is to provide people working in a specific domain with the possibility to model their part of the system, with their own vision, therefore in their own meta-model. We think of it as of a **modeling component**, because it has a private part, in which we place all we know of our domain, and a public part in which we present the elements we want other domains to see, i.e. the local solutions that fit in the global view. The component interface is specified by the domain meta-model.

The second part of our structure consists of **analysis models**. As their name suggests, these components provide analysis capabilities through the use of a meta-model. As input, they take models of a certain format, i.e. conforming to a specific meta-model, and they output the result of their analysis. They are the location of cross-cutting/non-functional properties validation.

Possible configurations are tested and local solutions not conforming to constraints are discarded. Between these two kinds of models, **adaptation models** establish a connection. Since all information is primarily available in domain models, we have to build the analysis models from them. This can be assimilated to **transformations** from the domain meta-models to the analysis meta-model.

We define adaptation models as the location that encapsulates these transformations, and provides the missing link between domain models and analysis models.

Figure 9.1 shows an example of how models can be structured. Modeling components at the bottom are domain models; they contain the data for *Hardware*, *Software* and *Mechanical engineering* facets of the system.

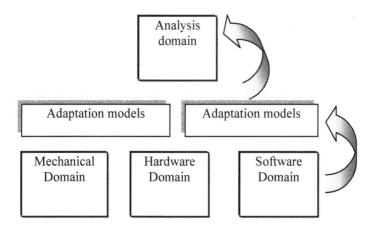

Figure 9.1. *General view*

The analysis manages two properties: **Codesign** and **Space management**. Among other things, we check that software and hardware are compatible, and that the envelope of the device is spacious enough to accommodate the hardware. The meta-model used to validate these properties is different from the ones of the domain models.

Adaptation models *Codesign* and *Space management* apply required transformations, and generate analysis data from domain data. Doing so, they perform an abstraction operation, since we are in a case where transformations do not add any information to the models.

9.2.4. *MDD Implementation*

9.2.4.1. *Presentation*

In order to implement this structure, we use a model-driven Web application generator called Netsilon (for further details, see [MSFB05]). Netsilon uses the combination of three models as the basis for generation into a Web application:

- A "Business Model" that abstracts the business concepts of the Web application;

- A "Hypertext Model" that describes the composition and navigation details of the Web application;

-A "Presentation Model" that contains the details of the graphical appearance.

Netsilon comes with an action language, Xion, through which we specify most of the behaviour of the application. This language is based on OCL, and is perfectly adapted to navigation into set-based data structures. It also provides action capability, with Java-like syntax. Thus, Xion has three types of features:

- Query capabilities, inspired by OCL, offer the possibility of querying a model and extract sets of elements conforming to given criteria;

- Constraint capabilities, inspired from OCL, provide the possibility to specify invariants, i.e. constraints;

- Action capabilities, added on top of the OCL-like basis, support the enforcement of constraints, through operations such as create/delete objects, modify values, process calculations on model elements, etc.

The models and their attached Xion code are translated into a full-featured Web application. The structure of the *Business Model* is transformed into a relational database, while the Xion code is translated into PHP routines.

The next chapter shows how we used Netsilon in conjunction with the proper structuration of models to produce a light, distributed, evolutive tool that supports our system development.

9.2.4.2. *Metamodel implementation*

Netsilon does not provide meta-modeling capabilities, as tools like GME (see [GME05] or Kermeta (see [MFJ05]) do. However, we define a meta-model layer: we declare our meta-classes to be abstract classes in Netsilon. We consider inheritance between abstract classes on the one side and "normal" classes on the other side is a valid way of separating the two levels. In this respect, we apply the meta-modeling views of Atkinson and Kühne (see [AK01]), by implementing attributes and methods with high potency. Table 9.1 shows how we organise levels of abstraction to get the functioning we want.

OMG Notation	Abstraction Level	Netsilon constructs
M2	Meta Model	Abstract Classes
M1	Model	Classes
M0	Instances	DB Entities

Table 9.1. *Organisation of abstraction layers*

In Figures 9.2 and 9.3, we see the distinction made between meta-model elements, "Physical_element" or "Device" for example, and model elements "Sensor" or "Piston".

9.2.4.3. *Tool prototyping*

In the example given, several types of meta-models are defined, as described below:

– Domain meta-models:

- Core domain meta-model: collection of general concepts used in all other domain meta-models;

- Hardware domain meta-model: concepts to model hardware architecture;

- Software domain meta-model: concepts to model software architecture;

- Mechanics domain meta-model: concepts to model a mechanical architecture.

– Analysis meta-models:

- Co-design: analysis of software and hardware data, in order to check that the system reaches its real time requirements;

- Various dimensioning routines, helping the designer finding elements that fits his criteria.

– Adaptation/connection meta-models. Numerous adaptation models are necessary to connect analysis models' elements to domain models' elements. Each time we need to specify a relation between two elements, we have to describe it through such an adaptation model. This rule enforces separation between primary models (domain models), transformation models (adaptation models), and target models (analysis model).

This architecture of models provides designers with a repository in which to clearly specify their works. Transformations are separated from data, and raw data are separated from analysis data. Each designer has the possibility to specify his own functionalities that he will execute on the model later, to perform various analyses. In order to do so, he just has to specify the target and the way to reach the target from existing information. Doing so, he does not interfere with other designers, since he does not modify any common element.

It is very important that data provided by developers is read-only, in order to maintain consistency and continuity of their views of the system. Basically, data integrity must be guaranteed. The intermediate and final results of the calculations have therefore to be stored somewhere other than in the original element; this is the role of the analysis model. Complementary information about this structure can be found in [MTC04].

9.2.4.4. *Domain models*

Figure 9.2 shows an excerpt from the core meta-model. The concepts it includes are very general, but this diagram shows an interesting feature. These are elements that we define at meta-level; they are therefore abstract, but they contain operations that will impact on all their instances.

If we have a specification that says "the mass of the system should not be over 1,000 kg" for example, we will be able to check that this mechanical constraint is respected at any time through a call to the "checkMass" operation of "Physical_element".

We have the possibility to use an action language at meta-level. This allows us not only to specify constraints at meta-level, but also to specify the way we want this constraint to be enforced at lower level of abstraction.

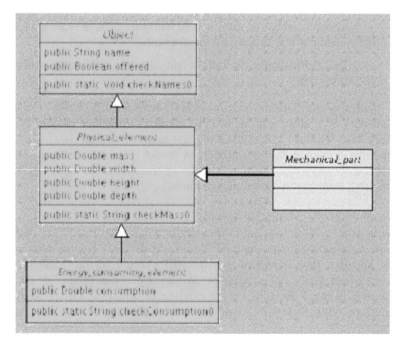

Figure 9.2. *Excerpt from the Core domain meta-model*

In Figure 9.2, we can notice that the "Object" entity, which is at the origin of all model elements, possesses an "offered" attribute. This feature is important: required objects are mirrors of objects developed outside of the scope of the domain, i.e. in another domain, but they impact on offered objects, which are developed within the scope of the domain. They are not really part of the domain model, in the sense that their existence there is specified by the designer, but their values come from elsewhere. One of the roles of the adaptation models is to control this data flow, but we will not describe this process here, because it is not really representative of our approach; it is just a side-effect.

Figure 9.3 shows the meta-model of hardware architecture (electronic cards), while Figure 9.4 shows the meta-model for the mechanical part of the project.

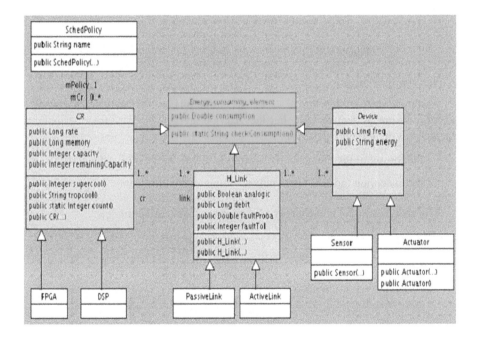

Figure 9.3. *Excerpt from the meta-model for Electronics*

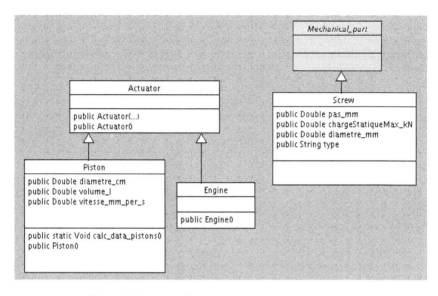

Figure 9.4. *Excerpt from the meta-model for Mechanics*

9.2.4.5. *Analysis models*

Analysis meta-models are *a priori* as numerous as the analysis we want to perform on our system models, but they can be merged for the sake of simplicity. An analysis meta-model describes:

- the format of the elements we need to gather to successfully run an analysis,

- the execution model of the analysis, implemented in Xion.

The analysis model is the target of a number of adaptation models.

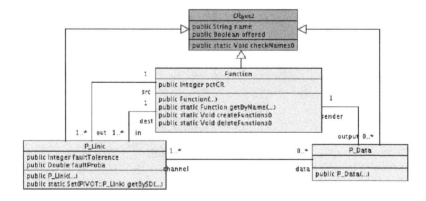

Figure 9.5. *Example of analysis model*

In Figure 9.5 we see a model meant to gather information on both software and hardware parts. By evaluating the consequences of the implementation of our processing on the hardware architecture step by step, we want to provide co-design support. The only limitation is the complexity of the techniques required to do so. In a first move, we implement only simple calculations, such as WCET approximate values, which are sufficient for discarding alternatives.

But we could have gone further, and even generate the model in a more adapted formalism if we had needed to.

The data for this model is extracted by adaptation models in the two domain models *Hardware* and *Software*. However, the information extracted from them depends on our intentions: the idea is not to copy systematically all elements from domain models into analysis model, not even to copy part of them.

We can modify the data "on-the-fly" in the adaptation model, so as to provide the analysis with already partly analysed data. The idea is therefore to specify a new data format that reflects our analysis policy.

9.2.4.6. *Adaptation models*

The meta-model of these models is very simple. It says that an adaptation element is linked to a number of domain model elements, to a number of analysis model elements and to a number of constraint elements. We define them in order to encapsulate the implementation of information flows and model transformations. This allows the domain models and the analysis models to be free of processing information. The typology of adaptation models we have identified is as follows:

- Mapping: it links elements from two or more domain models;

- Creation: it creates elements in one or more analysis models for each element or combination of elements in a domain model;

- Checking: it checks whether a constraint on a set of elements from one or several domain models is verified, and stores the result in an analysis model;

- Filter: it applies criteria on a set of elements from one or several domain models, and rejects those that do not pass the test. The rejection can be made through exclusion from the set, or through the deletion of the object;

- Computing: it computes a value on a set of elements from one or several domain models, and stores the result in an analysis model;

- Refactoring: it applies criteria on a set of elements from one or several domain models, and applies transformations to the elements that do or do not verify them.

By combining different types of adaptation models, we are able to obtain complex functionalities, such as dimensioning, decision-making or behavior verification. For example, to dimension a part of the system, given the rest of it, we define an analysis meta-model and then generate the analysis model from available elements of the domain models to finally generate the domain model elements that were missing, based on our analysis of the needs.

Following this pattern, we can automate a vast amount of processing, and capitalize them. Here is an example: we want to realize a float, and we specify an operational diving depth and a maximum diving depth.

Given that we have chosen to use a piston to manage the ballast, we want to select all known screws that can stand the pressure at maximum depth, and reject the others. The piston format being for us to choose, when the depth target depends on the maximum depth set in the specification, this filter will also allow us to make sure that our piston configuration is viable, i.e. that we have always at least one type of screw in the resulting set.

Figure 9.6 shows the structure of the adaptation model. We have gathered things that should have been separated for readability reasons. Indeed, we have on the same picture a combination of:

- an analysis model composed of "Screw_calc" and "Piston_calc";

- a mapping model that links "Screw" and "Piston" to their "*_calc" counterparts;

- a creation pattern that generates the "*_calc" elements from the domain models elements "Screw" and "Piston";

- a computing pattern that computes the maximum pressure and other characteristics for each "Screw_calc";

- a filter pattern that rejects the "Screw" elements whose associated "Screw_calc" element does not fit the requirement.

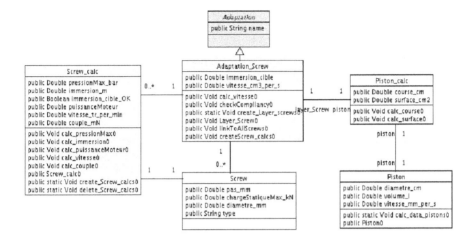

Figure 9.6. *Structure of the adaptation model filtering screws*

The Xion code for the selection of matching screws is composed of two parts: first, we make sure all data are up-to-date by computing them, then we filter the set of screws mapped to this particular filter through their associated "Screw_calc" (1-1 association). For each of them, we calculate the max acceptable pressure (based on the data we updated earlier), and check whether it is over the target max pressure with operation "calc_immersion", which sets the Boolean "immersion_target_OK". In case of failure, the element "Screw_calc" is deleted, which means that the corresponding screw is not linked any more to our evaluation model, but it has not been deleted, the screw data are intact in their original domain models.

In this particular selection processing, there is no need to retain the analysis model, but the computations realized for an adaptation model can be of some use to other adaptation models. When it is the case, the analysis model should not be deleted, because it is an intermediate between the domain models and a higher-level analysis model.

9.2.5. *System modeling framework conclusion*

First of all, this approach, coupled with the use of Netsilon, provides a light, distributed, configurable interface enabling storage of artefact information into a database, and validation. This is done by cutting out the model of the system by domain. Each specialist has its own personal model to work with, without interference from the outside. Each specialist therefore has the possibility of specifying tests or calculations to execute on his own domain model. The domain models are encapsulated in a modelling component.

The handling of the connections between domains (dependency relationships) through adaptation models enables mapping, filtering and refactoring information to be precisely located.

Transformations are also encapsulated into these specific models, which avoids primary models (domain and analysis) to be "polluted" with this information.

The creation of viewpoints for model analysis, enabled through the coupling analysis models/adaptation models, allows us to extract the essence of the project, which is useful for project management. A limitation is that our approach supposes that the granularity of models is never to change; this is why we can consider our meta-models stable.

Above all, this little application is an example of the power of using an action language at meta-level.

Through the specification of an execution model at meta-level in Xion, we transfer a bigger part of the specification process to the meta-model, and we therefore constrain the model much more effectively.

The constraints can be checked out dynamically during the operations of model transformations or value evaluations of the analysis model. The action language constitutes the base of the expression of model transformations, constraints and operational semantics of the meta-models, without being particularly close to any potential deployment language.

9.3. Building models for formal verification

The central objective of the verification process is the apprehension and analysis of a model of system according to reliability and temporal performances points of views. That resides in a double need as the handling of the domain models from the component which describes the dynamic behavior of the entities (these entities are in respect to the functional part) and the platform component which provides the communication link characteristics and an abstraction of the execution platform of the dynamic entities. This modeling component must include the real-time performances aims at the evaluation of the behavior of models, taking into consideration requirements specified by the designer. We say that the selection of whole of these necessary concepts, coming from several modeling components, constitutes a view characterizing the validation point of view of the system.

This view can be built via the adaptation models. The objective of this point of view is to determine if the system architecture allows that the executions defined in the functional views are realized in time and on the right data.

9.3.1. *Functionalities of the environment under development*

We are designing an infrastructure (Figure 9.7) to specify models. It must integrate meta-models to capture functionality and architectural aspects of the system but also requirement and operational configurations. The framework we choose to develop is based on those functionalities and principles: import and manipulation of models with several metamodels (UML2, AADL, SDL), integration and/or connection with existing tools (integration in an Eclipse framework), connection to formal model validation tools (OBP [DR06] and Ifx [BoGr02]). We point out that the objective is to have a study framework to experiment the formal techniques of checking industrial models. All the ideas hinted at in this chapter are still under development. Nevertheless, the state of the platform allows us today to lead proofs of an embedded model of avionics software. Thus, the environment which we currently are developing makes it possible: i) to import partial SDL models and to translate them into models IF, ii) to express behavioral properties and operational contexts coming from the requirements and to translate them into observer automata IF, iii) to carry out the properties verification by an analysis of reachability.

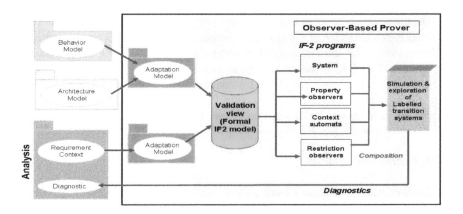

Figure 9.7. *A validation model framework*

9.3.2. *Observer and context-based model checking*

Our checking approach uses observers to express properties. This choice induces a limit as far as expression is concerned because an observer can only express safety, bounded liveness or reachability properties. However, this choice enables the user to describe with the same formalism the system to be validated and the properties to be checked on the system. To carry out the checking of a property, we will need to make an analysis of the reachability and to implement a synchronous composition between the system and the observer.

An observer [ABL98, HLR93] is an entity that follows the behavior of the system in order to check the failures of them. It is specified in the form of an automaton, which is strongly composed with the system to analyze. It is built so as to encoder a logical property and as a role to observe all the significant events related to the property that we wish to check. The observer automaton executes synchronously with the system and monitors run-time state and events of the observed system. It has special nodes known as *reject*. If one of these nodes is accessible during the composition of the observer with the system to check, then the property is not verified.

More precisely, to check a system S composed of several communicating timed automata with an observer O, the process is as follows. The observer O is associated S by means of a synchronous composition $(S\|O)$. An analysis of reachability of the reject[1] states is carried out on the product of this composition $(S\|O \text{ --> } reject)$. If one of these states is reachable, the property is not verified. If, on the contrary, none is reachable, the property is true.

The observer we have described is a non-intrusive observer. It observes and does not modify the behavior of the system. Another type of observers can be composed with the system for the checking. The restrictive observers block certain ways of exploration. This type of observer aims at limiting the space of exploration during the reachability analysis. The context automata are intrusive and interact actively with the system. We will see, in section 9.3.8, that each one of these types is established in language IF-2 using annotations and particular operators.

9.3.3. *Verification contexts*

Another important issue of our approach is the use of the checking contexts. Indeed, describing property on a system means to describe the behavior expected of the system in a given context. We choose therefore to check a property, to specify a

---

[1] A reject state is a state of accessibility graph corresponding in a reject node of the observer automaton.

context corresponding to the environment of the system. We have first identified a language to describe contexts called *α-contexts*, which makes it possible to describe a particular configuration of the system environment for which we wish to check a property. An *α-context* is an automaton whose transitions are abstract actions, named *α-actions*. These actions can be interpreted by the execution of a whole of elementary actions. This *α-context* is transformed by an operation of unfolding and by taking into account the elementary actions in a context called concrete context.

This generated context is then composed with the system at the same time of the observers. The advantage to this technique is to limit the behavior of the system associating it to this configuration represented by the context. So, this technique contributes to overpass the state explosion problem. Indeed, with the data events the context exchanges with the system, only active a subset of the system behaviors.

9.3.4. *Model transformation techniques*

The software framework (Figure 9.7), OBP (*Observer-Based Prover*), under development uses the checking technique based on observers described here. The tool is nowadays able to read the description of the system under validation, observers and *α-contexts*.

In the context of the system modeling framework based on modeling components, an adaptation model can imported in UML format, for example, from the software modeling component and transformed to IF-2 model. Semantic choices were made to have translatable models in timed automata based on a formal model.

For this, translation rules were identified and their implementation is under development with the Kermeta environment [MFJ05]. For the UML model transformation, the choice of the sub-set of the metamodel to be taken into account was necessary to enable the translation in IF and the choice of a semantic was made [Fag05] taking account of the Omega project results [ObGr03].

9.3.5. *A language to specify contexts*

When developing industrial software, the specification of contexts is not an easy task because it must take into account the whole set of behaviors, which can be numerous, of the framework system. On a life size system, it is useful to structure the description of the contexts. Thus, the observers are not easy to write if the property to check depends on the state in which the system is at the time we look for the value of the verdict. The system, according to those functioning modes, does not necessarily check the same properties. For example, an elevator does not have to answer a call from a floor during the maintenance process. We tried to couple the observers with the context in a same high-level specification in order to bring comfort of description for the user. At the same time, considering high-level specifications of course brings other advantages: a global view of the requirements on the system or possibilities for widespread traceability. To do so we inspired ourselves with the work of Jon Whittle [Whi05] who suggested the *Use Case Charts* (UCC). We intend to extend this formalism by the CxUCC (*Context eXtended UCC*) to integrate the description of the contexts and observers.

9.3.5.1. *Use Case Charts (UCC)*

[Whi05] introduces *use case charts*, a 3-level notation based on extended activity diagrams. The purpose of UCC is to simulate use cases and provide sufficient precise information and formal semantics so that a set communicating finite states machines can be generated automatically. A UCC is a specification with 3 levels. In level 1, an extended activity diagram is described where the nodes are use cases. In level 2, a set of extended activity diagrams identifies nodes as scenarios. A set of interaction diagrams, which conform to UML2, is described in level 3. In [Whi05], the syntax and the semantics are precisely described. The benefits of this formalism are to provide an easily understandable support to specify requirements and a precise notation that can be directly executed.

9.3.5.2. *An extension: the Context eXtended Use Case Chart (CxUCC)*

In our approach, the Whittle's UCC are extended including a context notion with the 3-levels description. An extended use case chart (Figure 9.8) describes the environment context of the system at the level 1. It describes the environment behaviors according to plan. At level 2, the scenario diagrams accept 3 kinds of final nodes: *ok* (normal), *cancelled* and *stopped*. We add at this level 2 observation diagrams to specify the properties and restriction with the observer automata format. The property observers to be verified or restriction observers to be applied on the system are linked to the environment behavior. An observation diagram is specified with UML2 state chart formalism for which we have limited the syntax and prescribed rules writing. The action language that we are prototyping in our study is inspired by action language proposed in the OMEGA project. In a CxUCC, the reference to a property observer links a level 1 node to this level 2 observer thanks to *property* stereotype. In the same way, a restriction is linked to a level 1 thanks to *restriction* stereotype. In these cases, each observer is described at the level 2 by an observation diagram.

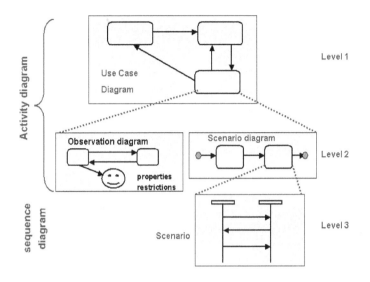

Figure 9.8. *Context eXtended Use Case Chart (CxUCC)*

To restrict the environment execution of the system to be checked, it is necessary to restrict actions specified in a context. For this, we implement an iteration count of the context by a generation of *counters*. These are initialized with values specified by the user in the CxUCC. These values result from the user experience and user knowledge of the system or from simulation results.

Semantically, as described in [Whi05], control flow of the entire use case chart starts with the initial node of CxUCC level 1. When the flow passes into a node at level 1, the linked scenario chart is executed. In the similar way, when the flow passes into a node at level 2, the linked scenario at level-3 is executed. In our scenario charts (level 2) there are three types of final nodes: i) a node *ok* represents successful completion; ii) a node *cancel* represents completion with failure. In this case, the flow passes again into the beginning of the scenario chart if it is possible in respect to the configuration of counter values, iii) a node *stop* represents completion with failure and the scenario chart execution stops.

We choose the semantic of observation diagrams as that of timed automata. The observers are implemented in respect to the *activation* principle. It consists of activating an observer (restriction or property) only when the flow passes into the node on which it is linked. It allows the observer to be activated only during the context execution connected to it. The facility is proposed to the user to describe his observers independently of the context. We think that it simplifies the specification of the observers. For the implementation, the observer automaton receives a specific signal when the connected scenario diagram begins its execution. In the same manner, when the scenario chart terminates, the observer automaton is stopped by the signal reception from the context. This allows an observer to become active during the execution context period. This mechanism is transparent for the user and is implemented automatically during the IF-2 programs generation.

9.3.6. *Translation of CxUCC to observers and concrete contexts*

The CxUCC are translated to a set of contexts and a set of observers. For this, the translation implies the following steps (Figure 9.5): i) the translation of a CxUCC to an α-*context* and a set of observers, ii) the unfolding of the α-*context* to an environment (or *concrete*) automaton, iii) and then the split of the unfolded automaton into a set of *path* automata. Finally, each generated path can be translated to IF-2 automaton and composed with the system automata to be checked and the observer automata. The reachability analysis is computed on the result of this composition. If a reached *reject* state of a property observer for one path exists, at least, then the property is not verified.

9.3.7. *Translation of CxUCC to an a-context and an observer set*

The translation principle of CxUCC to α-context is as follows: the scenario diagrams are translated to α-actions, then, the level 1 diagram to an α-context. The actions of this α-context are the α-actions generated previously. In a scenario diagram, each possible execution generates an elementary execution. Each one is marked with the final label *ok, cancel*, or *stop*. The concurrent executions specified in the level 1 diagram (*fork/join* multiples transitions and concurrence flag *) are translated to the complete interleaving of α-actions. An observer diagram is translated to a timed automaton taking in account the activation messages.

To restrict the unfolding, and so to limit the execution path number explosion, the unfolding algorithm takes into account the counter values whose the initial values are been specified by the user in the level 1 CxUCC diagram.

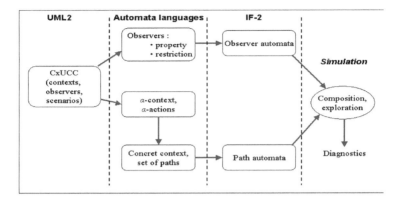

Figure 9.9. *Transformation of CxUCC to timed automata*

9.3.7.1. *Unfolding of a-context to concrete context*

The unfolding consists of replacing each α-action by the elementary action set that defines it. This unfolding is controlled by taking into account the set of counter values, to ensure the ending of concrete context generation. The unfolding of the α-*context* in Figure 9.10 (a) is presented in Figure 9.10 (c) as an example of the system. Figure 9.10 (b) shows an intermediate step of the unfolding with the counter values.

9.3.7.2. *Path set generation*

The context creation to handle verifications contributes to circumvent the combinatory explosion. However, it is not enough with large size systems. In fact, a context can contain several thousand paths. So, we propose a state space split of system connected to a context to a path. This technique allows the contexts to be split into a set of independent paths. These paths can be explored separately in respect to the safety and reachability property preservation.

All the behaviors of the system connected to each path correspond to the behavior of the system connected to the α-context. The concrete context generated in the previous phase is a cyclic automaton and finite thanks to initial bounded values of counters. The set of the executions described by the paths corresponds exactly to the execution set of concrete context. Figure 9.11 shows the path set of automaton in Figure 9.10 (c).

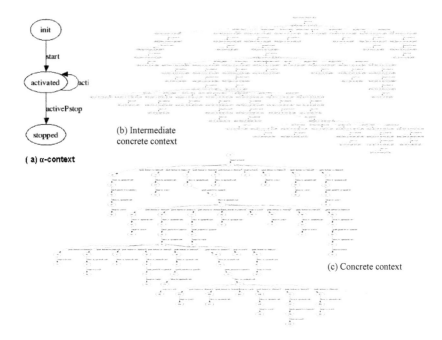

Figure 9.10. *Unfolding of a-context (a) to concrete context (c)*

Figure 9.11 shows the generation result of paths to be composer with system and observers automata for the example.

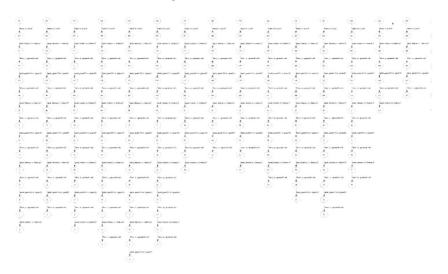

Figure 9.11. *Path automata generated (partial view)*

9.3.8. *IF-2 implementation*

The choice of the implementation language of the models and the observers was made on the language IF-2 [BoGr02] for which many tools were developed. They allow the programs IF and transitions systems to be generated from other languages (for example, SDL, LOTOS, etc.) in order to carry out formal properties checks. The IF processes are communicating timed automata by messages buffers. The communication channels implemented in this language can be parameterized to specify the type of communication (*multicast, unicast, peer*), the quality of the media (*reliable, lossy*), the type of plug (*fifo, multiset*) and the temporization of the communication (*urgent, delay, rate*). Advanced data structures allow a fine description of the systems in IF. The simulator of models IF makes it possible to generate a reachability graph representing the set of all the possible executions of the model. Time in these graphs can be represented in two manners: with discrete time, where the progression of time is simulated by tics of time and each clock has a value. In dense time, the progression of time is implemented by a progression transition and the set of the clocks is characterized by DBMs (Difference Bound Matrices) [AD94]. VERIMAG developed tools with IF for analysis static of the models such as *slice* or *live*, able to carry out a consequent reduction of the models before even the execution of the system. The toolkit CADP [Fern96] carries out analyses (*evaluator*, *xtl*), bisimulations, reductions and abstractions (*Aldebaran*) on the generated graphs of reachability. VERIMAG provided libraries, *model* and *simulator*, which makes it possible to the users to adapt the design of utilities like code generators or reachability graphs explorers. *Model* makes it possible to read a system written in IF and to manage a syntactic tree in memory. *Simulator* is an essential tool for the realization of explorer of reachability graphs of models IF.

The different kinds of observers described in section 9.3.2 are established by annotated processes IF observers [ObGr03]. Both kind of observers, property or restriction, defined previously are characterized in IF by the key words: *pure* for the first and *cut* for the second (restrictive). They monitor the system with the *match* instruction able to detect the occurrence of the signals of the system. It is important to note that the processes observers have priority upon which system to validate. Indeed, the IF automata communicate using buffers; however, observers need to be strongly synchronized with the system. Their priority level thus allows this synchronous composition. Moreover, IF allows nodes *error* and nodes *success* to be defined. The property observers are defined with IF *pure observers*. The marked nodes *error* make it possible to give a verdict, while the nodes *success* make it possible to stop the reachability analysis (as a restriction) in a path when arrived in a state considered successful (option "*cut one success*" of the simulator). The restrictions are expressed in IF with cut *observer*. These observers can block the reachability analysis in some path using the *cut* instruction, but they do not contain either *error* or *success* nodes. Their role is to reduce the reachability graph, and not to check a property. So, the context automata are generated using classic process IF, transforming an open system to a closed one. For each generated path, Table 9.1 presents the complexity of the exploration graph (states and transitions number) after composition of each path with system automata, property *car arrives on call* observer and the restriction observer. In this verification, the property is verified for each path.

Path number	States	Transitions	Path number	States	Transitions
1	693	1266	15	277	506
2	646	1181	16	323	590
3	693	1266	17	369	675
4	739	1350	18	415	759
5	785	1434	19	462	844
6	739	1350	20	369	675
7	508	928	21	138	253
8	462	844	22	92	168
9	508	928	23	138	253
10	554	1012	24	184	337
11	600	1097	25	231	422
12	646	1181	26	277	506
13	554	1012	27	184	337
14	323	590			

Table 9.2. *Exploration graph complexity after composition*

9.4. Conclusion and future work

This chapter has presented a model management approach and a validation process based on observer.

In the first part, we discussed the importance of model management and showed that it was possible to generate such a tool with the support of executable meta-models. We presented a ternary structure composed of 1) domain models for system developers, 2) analysis models for project managers, and 3) adaptation models to encapsulate mappings and transformations. This structure of modeling components, combined with the expressiveness of Xion, Netsilon's action language, enables a management framework for system models. Through the use of an action language at meta-level, we allowed the methods of meta-entities to have a very wide scope in underlying models. In this framework, the role of the meta-entities is enforced due to the executability of the meta-level.

In the second part of the chapter, we presented an experimental language, named Context eXtended UCC (CxUCC), to describe contexts, properties and restrictions in the same language as activity diagrams and sequence diagrams. We derived context automata from extended use case charts produced at the end of the analysis development stage. This early use of these diagrams is important to capture sequential dependencies between use cases and allows contexts to be generated automatically. In this study, we wanted to design a methodology for model validation and our experimentation was being implemented in the OBP environment. The specification of the system contexts to be composed with the system model can be a solution to circumvent the behavior complexity. Semantic choices were made to have translatable models in timed automata based on a formal model. Actually, the ideas presented in this chapter are experimented on a communication protocol model in avionics domain. This protocol is modeled with SDL, but this experience can be extended to UML2 or AADL models.

In the goal to have a complete MDD approach for formal validation on embedded systems, we plan to integrate the model management framework based on executable metamodels and the CxUCC language to generate the contexts and the observers. This development will be performed in the Eclipse framework with the Kermeta Plugin. Kermeta is a metamodeling language developed in the Triskell/INRIA team [MFJ05]. This language is used to describe the metamodels and to implement the necessary model transformations. This set of transformations must implement the MDD process for formal validation applying to embedded systems.

9.5. References

[ABL 98] L.Aceto, P.Bouyer, A.Burgueno, and K.G. Larsen. Model checking via reachability testing for timed automata. In Bernhard Steffen, editor, TACAS'98, volume 1384 of Lecture Notes in Computer Science, pages 263--280. Springer-Verlag, 1998.

[AD 94] Alur R, Dill D, A Theory of Timed Automata, Theoretical computer Science, 126(2):183-235, 25 April 1994.

[AK 01] Colin Atkinson and Thomas Kühne. The essence of multilevel metamodeling. UML 2001, 2001.

[Apv 04] L.Apvrille, JP.Courtiat, C.Lohr, P.De Saqui-Sannes, TURTLE : A real-Time UML Profile Supported by a Formal Validation Toolkit, IEEE Transactions on Software Engineering, Vol. 30, No7, pp 473-487, July 2004.

[BoGr 02] M. Bozga, S. Graf, and L. Mounier. IF-2.0: A validation environment for component-based real-time systems. In Proceedings of Conference on Computer Aided Verification, CAV'02, Copenhagen, LNCS. Springer Verlag, June 2002.

[DR 06] Ph.Dhaussy, JC.Roger, Un assistant de preuve basé sur la technique des observateurs, conférence AFADL'06, 15-17 mars 2006, Paris, 2006.

[Fag 05] U.Faghihi, Ph.Dhaussy, J.Champeau, JC.Roger Transforming UML models to communicating extended timed automata system IF, research report, ENSIETA-Université Rennes I, June 2005.

[Fern 96] JC. Fernandez et al., CADP: A Protocol Validation and Verification Toolbox, in R.Alur and T.A. Henzinger, editors, Proceedings of CAV'96 (new Brunswick, USA), Vol. 1102; LNCS, August 1996.

[GME 05] GME user's guide. Technical report, 2005.

[HLR 93] N.Halbwachs, F.Lagnier and P.Raymond. Synchronous observers and the verification of reactive systems. 3rd int. Conf. on Algebraic Methodology and Software Technology, AMAST'93, June, 1993.

[MSFB 05] Pierre-Alain Muller, Philippe Studer, Frederic Fondement, and Jean Bézivin. Platform independent web application modeling and development with netsilon. Journal on Software and Systems Modeling, 2005.

[MTC 04] François Mekerke, Wolfgang Theurer, and Joel Champeau. Non-functional aspects management for craft-oriented design. Workshop on Non-functional aspects of Component-based Software 2004, UML 2004, 2004.

[MFJ 05] PA.Muller, F.Fleurey and JM.Jézéquel, Adding Execution in Meta Model, 8th Int. conf. MoDELS 2005, Montego Bay, Jamaica, October 2005.

[ObGr 03] Iulian Ober, Susanne Graf and Ileana Ober. Validating timed UML models by simulation and verification. SVERTS'03, San Francisco, USA, October 2003.

[St 05] Friedrich Steimann. Domain models are aspect-free. MODELS 2005, 2005.

[Whi 05] Jon Whittle. Specifying precise use cases with use case charts. In MoDELS'05, Satellite Events, pages 290–301, 2005.

CHAPTER 10

The Design of Space Systems

An Application to Flight Software

Chapter written by David Chemouil

CNES
Avenue Edouard Belin
31401 Toulouse Cedex 9 – France
www.cnes.fr
david.chemouil@cnes.fr

10.1. Introduction

10.1.1. *Context*

This article deals with Space Systems and the way they are designed, as far as Software Engineering is concerned. Here, however, "software" should be taken in a broad sense, as the boundaries between software, hardware or systems matters may be rather tight on some aspects. This is not to say that every discipline reduces to the others but rather that they share, at some point, what may be coined as a "discrete" or "digital" representation of information. Hence, the design techniques and tools often look similar, and this similarity can be exploited so as to achieve better collaboration and to facilitate trade-offs.

Nonetheless, it is important to say that, until now, designing Space Systems has mostly been a *craft*, i.e. the work of domain experts relying on their skills and on business knowledge. Supporting tools and methods have been proposed and used (e.g. the HOOD methodology [HOO 91]) but none really made their way through to a complete adoption. There are good reasons explaining this situation: most notably, the Space Systems domain is a *niche* (few, specific, projects led to *ad hoc* approaches); and, until very recently, the design of Space Systems was manageable enough to be handled by rigorous and seasoned experts, using software tools only occasionally and following a standard process. It should also be noted that the vast majority of Space Systems do not include manned vehicles, which lowers the criticality of applications (there is no notion of certification, either).

However, as many other businesses have been doing, the design of Space Systems is experiencing a so-called "Software Crisis": by this, we mean that the complexity of systems requirements increases in such a way that designing correct Flight Software becomes more and more intricate. To handle this, new *scalable* tools and techniques will become essential in the near future. It is a commonly agreed fact that (part of) this scalability can be achieved through modelling. (My personal view is that modelling is a condition to success but is not worth the hype without a mathematical background giving meaning to models, as for any engineering discipline: try designing the Millau Bridge without structural mechanics!)

10.1.2. *Outline*

This article is structured into three parts. The first section introduces Space Systems by presenting their applications and architecture. The second section details the design of such systems. A special emphasis on On-Board Software is given. Finally, the third section describes some directions currently followed by CNES and the spatial industry regarding modelling technologies.

10.1.3. *Notice*

Space Systems are big and very complex, and the variety of ways to address their design makes it hard to reach a common understanding and to devise a common view on the directions that should be followed. Henceforth, some people may not share all ideas expressed here. Furthermore, this article also tries to illustrate the *industrial* nature of the work being done. By this, it is meant that design decisions aren't always motivated by technical or scientific reasons. Note also that this presentation is written with the French and European Space sector in mind. Some points may be wrong when considering other areas.

10.2. Space Systems

10.2.1. *Applications*

The Space Industry is rather young and relies on two branches. The first one is led by *agencies* such as CNES[1] or ESA[2]: in general, their purpose is, on the one hand, to develop scientific experiments and "societal" and defence applications; and, on the other hand, to promote the European Space Industry. The second branch is purely *industrial* and is an offspring of the first one: once a series of agency-led civil applications reaches maturity, it ceases to be an agency matter and becomes a commercial application directly sold by *prime contractors*.

Industrial applications mainly include telecommunication (telephone, video, etc.), and weather-forecast satellites. This is especially true of the first application, whose design and project management is now well known. Space Agencies may still participate in those applications but do not lead them anymore (they sometimes provide specific instruments, or special services such as handling the commissioning phase) as they succeeded in creating a living market.

Other Space Systems include applications that are either out of the scope of prime contractors (e.g. defence satellites) or considered as non-profitable, for the time being or forever. This area includes scientific applications (satellites or probes) such as: oceanography (Jason, Poseidon), space sciences (Sun observation: Soho, space observation: Herschel, Planck), space exploration (Mars Explorer, Venus Express), Earth sciences (earthquake detection: Demeter) and so on. Sometimes, a civil need may also be identified without entailing the creation of a whole commercial industry even if a small market may exist: Earth observation (Spot, Pléiades HR), Earth monitoring (fire detection: Fuego, environment evolution: Vegetation).

10.2.2. *Two Views on the Architecture of Space Systems*

The architecture of Space Systems is usually analysed using two different criteria. The first view stipulates that a system is characterised by big "functions" influencing its design and operating. The second view is classical and corresponds to the well-known recursive decomposition into modules down to components.

For the sake of comprehension, I chose to present the latter first, as it is topologically significant: nonetheless, it is important to emphasize the fact that

---

[1] The French Space Agency (CNES, centre national d'études spatiales) was founded in 1961 and contains around 2,500 employees.

[2] The European Space Agency was founded in 1975 and contains around 1,900 employees. It is funded by 17 Member States and is independent from the EU.

system architecture actually *follows from* functional architecture through a *mapping* decision (happening mainly during the first phases of the design process; see section 10.3.1.2).

10.2.2.1. *System Architecture*

A Space System is made up of 3 *segments*[3] that collaborate to perform one (or more) *mission*, that is, a given function. The next sections will give some details. However, note that this chapter mainly concentrates on the space segment.

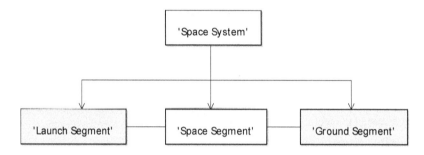

Figure 10.1. *Space Systems Decomposition*

10.2.2.1.1. Space Segment

The space segment contains one (or more) *spacecraft*[4]. Interestingly, various spacecraft simulators (whose representativity ranges from very abstract to extremely detailed, with actual components and hardware boards in closed loop) are also part of the space segment. They are used to carry out test and qualification activities, as well as software maintenance and update tests during lifetime.

---

[3] Notice that spacecraft prime contractors may speak about the spacecraft as the whole system, thus neglecting the influence of the interface between the spacecraft and the ground segment and the trade-off regarding the distribution of functionalities. This is a reason why the need for a concerned contracting authority, like an agency, is critical.

[4] I'll write "spacecraft" to mean a *satellite* but also a *probe*, or even a *lander*.

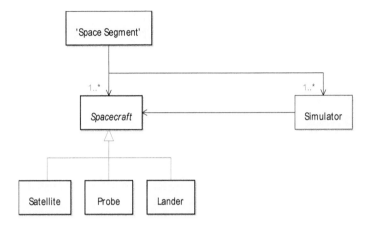

Figure 10.2. *Space Segment Decomposition*

Usually, a spacecraft contains a *platform* and a *payload*. The payload contains, among its *equipment*, one (or more) *instrument* and is in charge of one (or more) function (e.g. making pictures, detecting gamma rays, etc.) related to the mission; while the platform is in charge of giving means to the payload to fulfill its function and to the ground segment to manage the satellite.

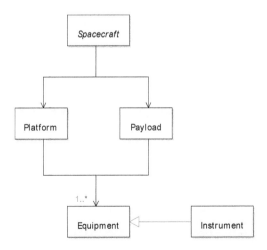

Figure 10.3. *Spacecraft Decomposition*

Now, a piece of equipment is made of different *elements*, each of them being constituted from *components*.

Figure 10.4. *Equipment Decomposition*

10.2.2.1.2. Ground Segment

The ground segment is in charge of maintaining the space segment to perform the mission with the best possible achievement. These two different functionalities are also strengthened by the contracting schema. This schema makes a distinction between the *client* who needs mission data and mission programming possibilities, and the *operating authority* whose work is to make the spacecrafts work correctly. Thus, two facilities are needed, namely a *mission centre* and a *control centre* (note that *ground stations* are also part of the ground segment, but are less interesting as far as functionalities are concerned).

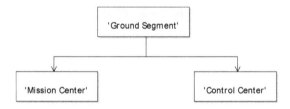

Figure 10.5. *Ground Segment Decomposition*

As an example, consider an observation satellite such as Spot: the client is a picture reseller (hence the client is not necessarily the end-user), namely Spot Image, and the operating authority is CNES. It is obviously not the role of CNES to decide which pictures should be made, and therefore a specific mission centre is needed to program them and send them to the instrument on the satellite. The mission centre should also receive picture, that is, mission data (under the form of PLTMs; see section 10.2.2.2.1), directly. On the other hand, it is the role of CNES to maintain the satellite safe, hence the need for a control centre emitting TCs and receiving HKTMs.

10.2.2.1.3. Launch Segment

Finally, the launch segment contains the *launcher* (that is, the rocket), as well as its control centre (not to be confused with the ground-segment control centre) and stations. Usually, several spacecrafts are embedded into the launcher and released almost at the same time, when the needed altitude is reached. Contrary to space-crafts, on-board software embedded into the launcher is mostly of avionic nature.

10.2.2.2. *Functional Architecture*

10.2.2.2.1. Functional Decomposition

Business experts usually speak about *functional chains* to describe sets of func-tionalities provided by equipment and/or software distributed among the system:

- Mechanical chain: manages the mechanical structure (mechanical interfaces, volume, vibrations, etc.) of the spacecraft;

- Mission chain: programs mission actions through MPOs (*mission-plan or-ders*, also called "macros"), provides mission data through PLTM (*payload telemetry*) and manages the payload;

- Power chain: manages the generation, storage and distribution of electricity in the spacecraft; also deals with Electro-Magnetic Compatibility (EMC);

- Thermal chain: maintains good thermal conditions on equipment;

- Attitude-and-orbit control chain: maintains the spacecraft attitude and orbit[5];

- Control-command[6] chain: manages data flows through TC (*telecommands*) and HKTM (*housekeeping telemetries*) and data storage on-board; and deals with operating *modes* of the spacecraft and on-board *processings* as well as FDIR[7] strategies.

10.2.2.2.2. Functional-Chain Mapping

It should be noted that the mapping from functional chains to spacecraft equipment is not necessarily one-to-one (though it is often the case): for in-stance, a star-observation instrument obviously belongs to the mission chain, but also to the AOCS one, should it be used as a "star tracker" providing data aimed at attitude control.

---

[5] The orbit is the trajectory followed by the spacecraft while its attitude is the direction pointed at by the spacecraft. Few spacecrafts can change their orbit autonomously.

[6] A word of caution here: "control-command" carries many meanings varying according to the industrial context and the language. It is therefore preferable to say that, as far as our Space Systems are concerned, control-command deals with *operating* the spacecraft (through TC) and *observing* it (through HKTM).

[7] FDIR: Failure Detection, Isolation and Recovery.

People use the word *subsystem* here, which means a functional, rather than topological, assembly of equipment implementing a functional chain, but where a given piece of equipment may participate in several functional chains.

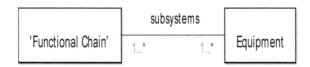

Figure 10.6. *Mapping between Functional Chains and Equipment*

10.3. Design

This section deals with how Space Systems are designed. However, the reader should recall that all design processes and requirements differ from one system to another. This section is also written with on-board software business in mind: some systems' questions, though important, are simply not taken into account.

10.3.1. *Process*

10.3.1.1. *Stakeholders*

10.3.1.1.1. Customer vs. Supplier

As in many businesses, stakeholders cannot be discriminated according to a technological criterion only. In fact, there is firstly a commercial partition which does have consequences on the design.

The common way to deal with such a situation is to speak in terms of *customers* and *suppliers*. For a given product belonging to the Space System, a customer may have a supplier but, then, every such supplier may also be a customer from another supplier's perspective.

This recursive decomposition applies everywhere: the end-user (you!) is a customer for a picture provider (Spot Image), who is itself a customer for a contracting authority (CNES), who is itself a customer for a satellite prime contractor... In the end, a whole development may involve several dozens of companies.

10.3.1.1.2. Engineering

Engineers participating in design belong to various companies and the actual organisation will vary from one project to another.

In any case, we will find *system engineers*, but this term carries many meanings that should be made explicit. In fact, their precise role will vary:

- Some system engineers are responsible for a system or subsystem development. They must monitor the design, have a complete view of the system (e.g. the satellite, the payload, etc.), but are not designers *per se*. Furthermore, they have to deal with non-technical aspects (contracts, funding, diplomacy, etc.). Here, some general system models may help but will mostly act as helpful *drawings*. As authors, their main technical output is the *statement of need*;

- Some other engineers specialised in a certain field (structural mechanics, electronics, etc.) work as system engineers in that they participate in designing the system considered as a whole, dealing with a specific viewpoint. Here, system *interfaces* (i.e., boundaries, not software interfaces: power sockets, for instance), *redundancies* and abstract *laws* or *behaviours* are the main outputs under the form of *system user requirements* documents. SysML may find its way, provided it is enriched with adequate semantics reflecting specific matters (power distribution, thermal regulation, flight mechanics, etc.). However, the need for specific tools probably will not disappear: think about Matlab or Scilab for physics, or Catia for manufacturing.

Among these system engineers, *control-command engineers* are of particular interest to software engineers. Indeed, they deal with all "informational" (or "discrete", "digital", "symbolic") system requirements, that is:

– System expected functionalities (what should it do?).

– Operational modes for the system and subsystems. Typical modes include:

  - Normal mode, i.e. "do nothing" but stay balanced,

  - Safe mode(s), in case of important failure, waiting for ground intervention,

  - Mission mode(s) to perform the mission,

  - Thruster mode(s) to acquire or correct a specific orbit.

– "Electrical" interfaces (TM/TC format, hardware/software interfaces, including bandwidth, power or thermal matters)[8];

– FDIR strategies. A typical distinction is "fail-safe" mode vs. "fail-op" mode: the former means surviving a failure going into a safe mode while the latter is more involved as it implies staying in an operating, though degraded, mode (usual telecommunication satellite strategy);

– System validation and qualification;

– System database (SDB), which contain data relevant to all previous points, plus specific software data or functions;

– Trade-off between on-board vs. ground processings (which involves all previous items).

Obviously, many of these requirements trace down to ground and on-board software. This is particularly true of the latter because of all "low-level" issues that have to be managed by flight software.

A specific use of SysML would probably prove very interesting here but many items do not seem to be fully addressed yet, such as precise dependability matters (the AltaRica language [ARN 00] may serve as a useful basis in this respect) or the mapping from a SysML model to a software model or to another refined SysML model. AADL also seems well suited to certain aspects of control-command.

10.3.1.2. *Phases*

Reaching this section, the reader may feel like designing Space Systems must be a terrible mess... *E pur si muove!* Indeed, the design of products (system, subsystems, equipment, and so on) depends strongly on individuals, rather than formalised tools and methodologies. Nevertheless, the said individuals enjoy two characteristics:

- Extensive domain expertise;

- A formalised *process* insisting notably on reviews and *interface documents*.

---

[8] Hardware interfaces (I/Os), solely, number more than 10,000 parameters on a simple satellite.

The actual process may vary but usually follows the ECSS[9] process defined in ECSS-M-30A standard:

-   Phase A: Feasibility: sketching many solutions with their performances, costs, delays, etc., then choosing one;

-   Phase B: Preliminary Design: elaborating various system and subsystems requirements specifications;

-   Phase C: Detailed Design: designing the system;

-   Phase D: Integration and qualification: components are manufactured, integrated and tested. Through qualification, operators also learn how to use the system;

-   Phase E: Exploitation of the system, software maintenance and updates;

-   Phase F: Retirement: a satellite may either "fall again" and burn out in the atmosphere, or may be put on a "junk" orbit.

Phase A is usually preceded by a "phase 0" where the potential mission is analysed by experts through concurrent engineering facilities.

Obviously, each phase consists in many tasks. Phases C/D represent roughly 75% of design, while around 15% are carried out during phase E.

10.3.1.3. *Workflow*

Now, let us concentrate on phases C/D for flight software. Here, theoretical software lifecycle models apply: the resulting process is a "V lifecycle" with several increments. Increments correspond to modules of software managing a specific subsystem or providing the hardware abstraction layer and basic services. More precisely, these modules may themselves be divided into very few increments in case they are particularly complex or large.

Of course, whatever the increment is, there are steps corresponding to identifying requirements, then analysing them, then designing and coding a solution. Every such step is more or less worked out with refined solutions in mind, and AIT[10] is also prepared concurrently.

---

[9] ECSS: European Cooperation on Space Standardization (see http://www.ecss.nl).
[10] AIT: assembly, integration and tests.

10.3.1.4. *Documents*

10.3.1.4.1. Documents as Contracts

Looking back at section 10.3.1.1.1, the recursive customer-supplier schema may seem obvious and insignificant, but this situation has a huge importance when it comes to exchanging information; for this information is not only technically necessary (to be able to design the correct product) but also *contractual*. As such, the supplier's responsibility is engaged both *commercially*[11] and *legally*. Now, suppose some stakeholders exchange models (considered as contractual): in this situation, the notions of model *completeness* and *consistency* bear a stronger meaning, which should not be overlooked.

10.3.1.4.2. Product Documents

Product documents presented here only give a simplified version of the actual situation, centred on the production phases (other documents are obviously required, too; for example, those dedicated to validation). The obsolete ESA Software Engineering Standards (PSS-05-0 and others [PSS 91]) should be consulted to get a more realistic view. Anyway, they correspond to the workflow briefly described in section 10.3.1.3:

- System requirements: User Requirements Document (URD), Interface Control Document (ICD);

- Analysis: Software Requirement Document (SRD);

- General design: Architectural Design Document (ADD);

- Detailed design: Detailed Design Document (DDD).

10.3.2. *By the way, what is so special about Space Systems?*

Let it be said first and foremost: as far as the *design* of software is concerned, there is nothing especially new in Space Systems, at least nothing more special than in any other industry featuring software-intensive embedded systems. For all that, producing Space Systems is a hard task. This is mostly so because of some specific *requirements* and *constraints,* which provide a distinction with respect to other industries.

An important source of constraints relies in the nature of the spatial environment. Its characteristics vary greatly considering where the spacecraft is to be situated (its orbit). For instance, a spacecraft will endure electro-magnetical, thermal or me-

---

[11] For instance, tardiness in supplying a product to a client often translates into financial penalties; or, the notable quality of a product, or punctuality, results in special bounties for the supplier…

chanical disturbances: these may of course lead to a partial or total breakdown, but "small" disruptions are also the cause for numerous constraints on the design of the spacecraft. As an example, let us cite the thermal gradient which may amount to several hundreds of degrees, or solar wind, or magnetic storms, or varying attraction (depending on the density and shape of the Earth at a certain point), and so on.

As far as flight software is concerned, the main difficulties arise from dependability, operability and industrial constraints:

- Most of the time, the communication with a spacecraft is only intermittent, depending on visibility phases (the only exception being geostationary spacecrafts). For a low-Earth-orbit satellite like Spot, this may amount to a few dozens of minutes per day. There are two important consequences: the first one is the rather small amount of data communicable with the ground segment; while the second one lies in the inability for the ground to react quickly to an on-board anomaly (the spacecraft is therefore in the obligation to be at least able to remain in a safe mode, if not partially operating);

- Once a spacecraft has been launched, there is obviously no way to operate and observe it except through TC and TM. This implies that flight software should have been designed in a suitable way, such that it remains possible to operate the spacecraft in ways unforseen at the time of specification;

- Due to the radiative environment, hardware components are likely to have their registers modified from time to time, or even destroyed. This not only means that data in memory may be altered, but instructions too. This is particularly problematic when we consider the need to patch the software (either the executable in RAM or the image in flash memory). Finding good strategies (update protocols, EDAC [12], etc.) regarding this question is often a difficult task;

- Another aspect is that hardware is often limited compared to standard computers, both for what regards memory size and computational power (see Table 10.1). This can obviously have severe consequences on flight software, above all when many mathematical processings have to be carried out;

- Software validation is also a very difficult task, mostly because some parts of the system simply cannot be tested "for real" before launching. Various kinds of simulators are designed for every system, with different degrees of realism. Some of these help debug flight software (or vice-versa!) but some are also used to *qualify* the system, that is to check whether it is usable by operators (who have to be trained);

---

[12] EDAC: Error Detection And Correction.

- Finally, the whole lifecycle of flight software may last from 10 to 20 years. This is an issue as software designers usually do not keep following the same project for so many years, which may cause a loss of knowledge about the way the product works. This is even truer as it is rather frequent to fix flight software, but also to update significantly its specification and design, even when in flight.

	Processor	Power	Memory
Spot 4	F9450	0.7 MIPS	256 KB
Spot 5	MA3-1750	1 MIPS	512 KB
Pléiades HR	ERC32	13 MIPS	6 MB
Proteus	MA3-1750	1 MIPS	512 KB
Myriade	T805	4 MIPS	2 MB
Ariane 5	68020 68082	1.2 MIPS 222 KFLOPS	1 MB
Top cellular phone		100–300 MIPS	3–6 MB

Table 10.1. *Hardware Limitations*

10.3.3. *On-Board Software*

This section presents briefly various characteristics of flight software. It should be noted first that on-board software can be either *central* or *remote*, which means that we can find various pieces of software running on the central processing unit or on remote terminal units (e.g. a star-tracking software, a processing unit dedicated to the AOCS, a bus controller, etc.).

However, viewing current on-board software as distributed is a bit exaggerated, as every functionality is allocated as a whole on a single processing unit. The situation is expected to evolve in the near future, however (to improve performance), so modelling techniques for spacecraft on-board software should take distributed systems theory into account.

Currently, typical state-of-the-art central flight software counts between 50,000 and 200,000 lines of C or Ada code (until very recently, the assembly language was extensively used). It is admittedly small compared to other domains but it should be recalled that computational and memory resources are very limited. The main functions are derived from functional chains (cf. section 10.2.2.2.1) and comprise[13]: onboard "main" management (modes, management of other activities), power management, thermal management, AOCS management[14], mission management[15]. Control-command functions are often dispatched at every level of decomposition.

Regarding operating systems matters, the space industry usually uses so-called "real-time executives" (in-house developments, commercial software or free software such as RTEMS[16]). These are pieces of code statically linked to the rest of software and providing rather basic services: task management, scheduling, synchronisation and communication facilities, memory management, etc. However, "high-level" services (e.g. filesystem management, virtual memory) are not used (when provided).

Modern central flight software usually comprises around 10 to 20 tasks, a few of them being periodic (typical frequencies go from 1 Hz to 32 Hz), the others being sporadic or completely aperiodic. These tasks are generally managed through fixed-priority static scheduling (rate-monotonic style).

Payload software is a bit particular as it is usually very consuming on both computational and memory sides. This, and the fact that the system under development is the payload itself (and not the whole spacecraft), implies that this kind of software is distributed on the very payload. Though smaller than central flight software, payload software is very hard to develop:

-   A payload is often produced for one single mission, which makes it almost impossible for developers to gain a specific knowledge as to how it works;

-   External interfaces and behaviour may be very particular and badly specified;

-   Finally, it includes a lot of computation-intensive code (sometimes obtained by code generation from mathematical tools), some of which is highly aperiodic.

In summary, the reader is expected to understand that the hardest part in developing on-board software lies in the ability, or not, to verify and to validate it. It already happened to find very well-designed software that was almost unverifiable statically (this being due for instance to a large use of function pointers). Obviously, the most difficult tasks concern dynamic and per-

---

[13] Mechanical management is rather rare because it mainly relies on "passive" devices.
[14] This function is sometimes allocated to a remote unit.
[15] This function is often allocated to the payload itself.
[16] http://www.rtems.org

formance matters. Finally, FDIR is also problematic, as validating it means being able to guess possible failures and to simulate them (which is sometimes impossible, e.g. some solar array opening failures). Moreover, some FDIR strategies are so complex that they are almost impossible to validate (for this reason, for some satellites, there has been a movement towards using simple FDIR strategies, possibly needing ground intervention, rather than smart but hard to understand strategies).

10.4. Modelling

10.4.1. *Current Possibilities*

As far as modelling is concerned, there is no common agreement or working habits in the space industry. We already saw some of the reasons: this is a young industry, space systems remain "small" and "simple", etc. Another reason is that projects are organised in rather autonomous teams who choose their way to work on a project-by-project basis.

Nonetheless, it is a commonly agreed fact that the space industry remains well organised compared to other sectors, thanks to the ECSS processes. Furthermore, there is some experience on using modelling techniques, e.g. HOOD [HOO 91] but also a bit of UML [UML 04]. Admittedly, these languages have mostly been used for static design rather than specification or validation.

Some companies have, however, engaged a serious involvement in so-called Model-Driven Development, using software tools to design their on-board software completely and even generating part of the code. Unfortunately, even for design phases, UML (and tools) are not mature yet for fine design of real-time aspects (there is a profile, SPT, but it is poorly implemented in tools and seldom used anyway).

10.4.2. Trends and Projects

As far as CNES (together with partners from the space and other industrial businesses) is concerned, the aim is to devise a model-based development process for flight software and systems engineering, from the early inception to the latest validations. These both involve enhancing or designing modelling languages and, concurrently, carrying out methodological studies and recommendations.

The Topcased[17] project aims at developing a systems/software/hardware free-software modelling toolkit (built upon the Eclipse[18] editor). Apart from engineering matters, the main purpose is to design a tool and a method adapted to very long lifecycles (i.e. more than 30 years).

The background method is well-known and is based upon the "Y" lifecyle. This means being able to define "platform-independent models" (PIM) on the one hand and "platform description models" (PDM) on the other hand. PIMs should start with abstract models, then refined progressively towards a concrete one: this refinement chain should help making formal verifications providing confidence in the quality of the upcoming product. Taking the business domain into account may help automating these refinements and associated verifications. Weaving this last PIM with the PDM should produce a "platform-specific model" (PSM). This weaving might also be the result of some form of manual mapping description (instead of relying on an already given mapping). All these models should also be used to help validating the end product.

UML-style models, together with the upcoming MARTE[19] profile, tailored for flight-software business, may prove useful for the PIM part. The weaving function may be well addressed by the AADL, as well as systems models (describing the environment).

An important part of (future) flight software also lies in the dynamic-architecture design phase which happens early in the development, for pre-validation purposes. Distribution aspects are not taken into account so much currently but are expected to take a growing part in the near future: therefore, the deployment architecture will probably be important too.

As for code generation, some work is being carried out concerning Real-Time Java (through the RTSJ standard [WEL 01]), which is commonly thought to be the future implementation language for central flight software. One of the interesting parts of this language, compared to competitors, is its built-in dynamic-reconfiguration feature.

On the other hand, on a more prospective side, some work should be carried out to see whether and how synchronous languages could be integrated in flight software. Their advantages are well-known but their scope is somehow

---

[17] http://www.topcased.org

[18] http://www.eclipse.org

[19] http://www.promarte.org

in opposition with the AADL asynchronous point of view. The GALS[20] archi-tecture proposition might serve as a good starting point.

Similarly, at the boundary between systems and software, AADL and SysML may benefit from the AltaRica language, which offers very strong dependability analyses, more than necessary to systems engineering.

On another subject, we would like to point out the fact that requirement elicitation is still hardly taken into account by Model-Driven Engineering proponents (requirement models are just the outcome of this activity, not the activity itself). Some work has already been done, however, which can be witnessed through the *i** and KAOS methods. Engineers master more or less subsequent phases of the development, but user requirement elicitation is still poorly supported.

Finally, though it is already partly taken into consideration, verification and validation methods and tools should be well-defined and developed. On the one hand, models should be constantly checked, on the other hand, models should serve as V&V supporters (e.g. providing test oracles).

10.5. Conclusion

This article has dealt with the design of Space Systems, focusing largely on flight software. The aim was three-fold: firstly, to describe Space Systems architecture and applications; secondly, to present roughly the way systems and flight software are designed; and thirdly to discuss modelling technologies current in-and-outs and to give an indication on the directions followed by CNES and some of its partners.

This brief glimpse will hopefully have shown that the design of Space Systems, notably Flight Software, is indeed a hard task but also that there are many directions which, combined altogether, should provide means to scale up while improving the overall processes and products. Among these, Model-Driven Development *together with* Formal Methods for Embedded Systems are of prime importance.

---

[20] GALS: Globally Asynchronous, Locally Synchronous.

10.6. References

[ARN 00] ARNOLD A., GRIFFAULT A., POINT G., RAUZY. A, "The Altarica formalism for describing concurrent systems, Fundamenta Informaticae", vol. 40, p. 109-124, 2000.

[DAR 93] DARDENNE A., VAN LAMSWEERDE A., FICKAS S., "Goal-directed Requirements Elicitation", Science of Computer Programming, vol. 20, p. 3-50, 1993.

[HOO 91] HOOD TECHNICAL GROUP, HOOD Reference Manual 3.1, Noordwijk, European Space Agency, 1991.

[PSS 91] Software Engineering Standards, European Space Agency, 1991.

[REQ 97] YU E., Towards Modelling and Reasoning Support for Early-Phase Requirements Engineering, Proc. 3rd IEEE Int. Symp. on Requirements Engineering (RE'97), p. 226-235, 1997.

[UML 04] RUMBAUGH J., JACOBSON I., BOOCH G., *The Unified Modeling Language Reference Manual*, Addison-Wesley Professional, 2004.

[WEL 01] WELLINGS A., *Concurrent and Real-Time Programming in Java*, John Wiley and Sons, 2001.

CHAPTER 11

TOPCASED

An Open Source Development Environment for Embedded Systems

Patrick Farail[1], Pierre Gaufillet[1], Agusti Canals[2], Christophe Le Camus[2], David Sciamma[3], Pierre Michel[4], Xavier Crégut[5], Marc Pantel[5]

1: AIRBUS FRANCE, 316, route de Bayonne F-31060 Toulouse - France
2: C/S, ZAC de la Grande Plaine - Rue Brindejonc des Moulinais
BP 5872 - 31506 Toulouse Cedex 5 – France
3: Anyware Technologies, Prologue 2 - Rue Ampère
BP 87216 - 31672 Labège Cedex - France
4: FéRIA-ONERA, -DTIM, 2, avenue Edouard Belin
F-31400 Toulouse - France
5: FéRIA-IRIT-ENSEEIHT, 2, rue Charles Camichel,
BP 7122, F-31071 Toulouse Cedex 7 – France
www.topcased.org
{pierre.gaufillet,patrick.farail}@airbus.com

11.1. Introduction

The creation of industrial systems relies on numerous tools on which it is essential to capitalize in order to optimize development costs. However, the lifetime of critical systems such as aerospace products is often about 10 to 30 years, and currently, no software editor is able to commit for such a long time at an acceptable cost. To counter these risks, the CNRT [1] (National Center for Research & Technology) Aeronautic & Space partners started the TOPCASED project (standing for Toolkit in OPen source for Critical Applications and SystEms Development) which aims to develop an open source CASE environment with the following goals:

- to perpetuate methods and tools used for software developments,

- to minimize ownership costs,

- to ensure independence of development platforms,

- to integrate, as soon as possible, methodological changes and advances made in the academic world,

- to be able to adapt the tools to the process, and not the opposite,

- to take into account qualification constraints.

TOPCASED is now a project of the Aerospace Valley Competitivity Cluster, and gathers today some major industrial partners, like EADS Airbus, EADS Astrium, Atos-Origin, CS, Rockwell&Collins, Siemens-VDO, Thales Aerospace and Turbomeca; some SME like Adacore, Anyware Technologies, Micouin consulting, Sinters, Tectosages and TNI-Software; and some laboratories and schools: ENSEEIHT (repository of the collaborative development gforge platform for TOPCASED), ENSIETA, ESEO, ESSAIM, FéRIA-IRIT, FéRIA-LAAS, FéRIA-ONERA, INRIA Rhone-Alpes, INRIA-IRISA, the Federal University of Santa Catarina (UFSC, Brazil), the Paul Sabatier University (UPS).

This partnership is open. To become a new member and to participate to the strategic decisions, you will need to accept the TOPCASED membership charter, and your proposal will have to be validated by the steering committee. Of course, our tools remain publicly available.

The initial TOPCASED infrastructure developments have been funded by Airbus, and have been specified and implemented by Airbus, Anyware Technologies, CS and FéRIA. Only a small part of the full project has been addressed until now, mainly included in the WP2 – Modeling tools:

- SP2.1 – State of the art on modelling methods and languages

- SP2.2 – Meta-modelling language definition

- SP2.3 – Model editors specifications

- SP2.4 – Editor for the meta-modelling language

- SP2.5 – Editor for UML2 (currently use case and class diagrams)

- SP2.6 – Editor for AADL/COTRE.

This work led to the development of the first versions of the TOPCASED toolkit, which have been published through the project website (http://www.topcased.org) and the development server (http://gforge.enseeiht.fr).

Some work still need to be done on the improvements of the editors, on the development of new editors (EAST-ADL, SPEM and SysML developments are in progress) and on the semantics side of meta-models in order to enable the use of formal model validation tools. On the simulation side, a study is in progress that targets a generic simulation engine demonstrator for the end of 2006. A PhD has also been started at FéRIA-IRIT has started on the expression of the semantics of development processes at the meta-model level. A preliminary integration of OCL for the validation of models is also available. Many other points will be studied and developed during this project:

- WP1 – process and life-cycle for critical systems, which will provide a common process for the development of such systems taking into account the constraints and experiences of the various partners. All the concepts used in TOPCASED will be defined through a common ontology. The use of the MDA Y approach in system engineering will also be assessed. The WP1 tasks have already started;

- WP3 – model verification and simulation, which will makes it possible to integrate easily at the model level validation approaches based both on formal tools and simulations in the toolkit. A Ph.D. has started between FéRIA-LAAS and Airbus to work on pre-emptive software models verification;

- WP4 – implementation tools. This work package aims to select, and if required to improve and adapt to the qualification constraints the numerous implementation tools (GCC, binutils, GDB, CDT, JDT, etc.) already available in open source;

- WP5 – model transformations which will allow interconnecting the various tools and producing both code and documentation using the various models. Some tasks have been started at the end of 2005;

- WP6 – tools interoperability and data management. The first result of this work package is the current bus used by the TOPCASED tools. Some Stood (a HOOD software design tool) services have also been integrated to validate the connection of external tools to the toolset. This work package is in charge of transversal tools like anomalies management, requirement management, and version control systems. The first software tools should be published before the end of 2006 on these topics;

- WP7 – infrastructure. Three points will be studied in the WP7: the juridical point of view (what open source licenses are acceptable for the components we use, what open source licenses are acceptable for the components we release, software patents issues, insurance, copyright, etc.), the business model (who and in what conditions will the tools be maintained and developed, how to guarantee the perpetuity of the skills, etc.), and the technical means (collaborative development server, etc.). Some work has already been done on these 3 points;

- WP8 – safety. This work package has to specify on the one hand specific tools to ensure safety of the critical systems, and on the other hand to define some requirements on the other TOPCASED tools to ensure that they will have a positive impact on the final safety level of the products.

TOPCASED is today in touch with several other projects, like the Society of Automotive Engineers (SAE) Architecture Analysis and Design Language (AADL) standardization committee for AADL editors and analysis tools, the IST project ModelWare for the definition and the development of the ModelBus, the ATLAS group at INRIA, which is working on the ATLAS Transformation Language (ATL) used for our first implementations of models transformations, and the TopModL initiative, which aims to develop meta-modelling tools. Since the first release (October 2005), TOPCASED has been downloaded around 5,000 times.

11.2. Requirements and TOPCASED Architecture

The design of critical systems and softwares currently requires the use of many different models at various steps of both the system development process and its life-cycle. These models make it possible to express the various aspects of the system: both static and dynamic, functional and non-functional, at the systems and at the components level, software and hardware, clients and providers.

Many kind of tools have to be available to handle these models: textual and graphical editors; translators from one model type to another; code, test and documentation generators, version control systems, model validation tools.

The main technical requirement for a modern extensible and evolutive CASE tool is that it should be able to provide users with an easy access to the various models of a given system and to their associated tools. The TOPCASED project is based on Model Driven Engineering [10] (MDE) for this purpose:

- meta-modeling makes it possible to describe all the modeling languages in a common framework;

- model bus makes it possible to access easily to the various tools;

- model transformations make it possible to relate the various models and adapt models to the various tools involved in a project;

- generative programming makes it possible to easily produce both textual and graphical model editors;

- generic components decrease the tools development effort because they can be directly applied on nearly any modeling languages.

In the current industrial processes, these software tools will have clearly a more and more important place. Unfortunately, experience shows that it is really difficult for enterprises to keep mastering their software tools for the whole lifetime of their own products (a lifetime which can be as long as several decades). Indeed, the current industrial plan consists of sub-contracting the implementation and diffusion of the tools to specialized editors which are de facto the owners. Ownership problems usually arise when the interests of the industrial user and of the editor diverge, or when the editor is bought by another company or disappears, or when the technology evolves. It is mainly for this reason that the TOPCASED project has turned to free (like in freedom, not in costless) and open source software.

The fact that the tools documentation and source codes are open guarantees that it will be successfully maintained, possibly, in the worst case, at the price of creating a specific development branch, depending on the requirements of the industrial users. Working with open source software also brings some other advantages:

- it makes it possible to adapt the tools to the processes, where it is today required to do the opposite most of the time;

- the availability of the software interfaces ensures a good interoperability;

- the supported platforms are not limited, as is often the case, to the most common platforms at a given time;

- the tools and their source code being available, the academic actors can integrate very quickly their new techniques, and use the tools for the training courses.

The cost of the tools becomes the cost of development, deployment and maintenance, where today the most common proprietary tools are invoiced in proportion to the number of users. Moreover, this cost can be shared between the users, and reduced by the reuse of existing open source components. The implementation of the TOPCASED project relies on the open source plugin-based Eclipse CASE platform. The first tools developed are therefore Eclipse plugins. Nevertheless, the TOPCASED architecture also allows integrating smoothly external tools.

Of course, as TOPCASED addresses critical systems and software design, it has to take into account the processes which imply some products and tools qualification constraints, processes which are quite frequent in the embedded systems domain (DO-178B, DO-254, ECSS, etc.).

11.3. Model Driven Engineering and meta-modeling

The "*Object Management Group*" (OMG: http://www.omg.org/) was created in 1989 to provide frameworks and standards for the integration of object-oriented applications, mainly the CORBA [11] and UML [12] technologies.

The growing diversity of techniques and platforms used in software developments, as well as the emergence of non-CORBA based middlewares, like EJB from Sun and .NET from Microsoft, have taken the pre-eminent role away from CORBA. Then, OMG refocused its strategy and standards to support the MDA approach [13, 14]. MDA addresses the complete life cycle analysis design and programming aspects, providing an interoperability framework for defining modular and interconnected systems, and with the will to offer more flexibility in system integration and system evolution. A system design is organized around a set of models and a series of transformations between models, into a layered architecture. Central to MDA is the principle of defining different models at different levels of abstraction and linking them together to form an implementation. MDA separates the conceptual elements of an application from the representation of these elements on particular implementations technologies. For that purpose a distinction is made between "*Platform Independent Models*" (PIMs), representing the conceptual design of the application, and "*Platform Specific Models*" (PSMs) which are more solution oriented.

Transformations between models are key elements in the MDA approach: vertical transformations between PIMs and PSMs to express realizations, or horizontal transformations between PSMs for integration features. Underlying these model representations and transformations is the notion of "*meta-model*". The ability to express and transform models requires a rigorous definition of the (textual or graphical) notations supporting these models. Therefore, the notations to express models must themselves be described into models, which are called "*meta-models*". For example, the UML meta-model formally describes the notation of the different UML diagrams, so giving an unambiguous and precious common base to all tool providers and users.

The importance of meta-models has been recognized by OMG who proposed the "*Meta Object Facility*" (MOF). The MOF [14, 15] provides a meta-modeling hierarchy as well as a standard language for expressing meta-models. It proposes a structure of data in four different levels, so called the "*four-layer meta-model architecture*" (Figure 11.1):

- the bottom M0 level, or *Application level* gives the data values, i.e. the extension of an application,

- the M1 level defines the model, i.e. the intension for an application,

- the M2 makes it possible to define a schema, or language, for the application model: it is the meta-model level,

- the M3 level, or *MOF level,* proposes general concepts, defining the MOF meta-language, i.e. a schema for a meta-model: it is the meta-language level.

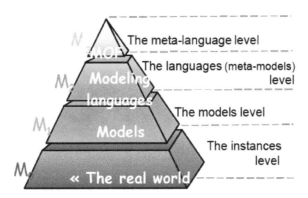

Figure 11.1. *The four-layer meta-model architecture*

The *four-layer meta-model architecture* is now widely accepted and was proposed (before the OMG MDA-MOF proposals) in other standards like the ISO/IEC standard for IRDS (*"Information Resource Dictionary System"*) [16] and CDIF (*"CASE Data Interchange Format"*) from EIA [17].

As TOPCASED relies on the Eclipse platform, the M3 meta-modeling language used is Ecore provided by the EMF (*"Eclipse modeling Framework"*) project [4] which is strongly related to Essential MOF 2.0 as specified by the OMG [15]. Several M2 modeling language editors have been developed (ECORE, UML2, SAM, and AADL) and others will follow (SYSML, SPEM, etc.). The M1 level then corresponds to specific system models (a UML use case, activity or class diagram) and the M0 level to instances of the models (a real execution of the system).

11.4. Generating model editors

As many different modelling languages are required, the production of model editors will be a key task for TOPCASED. Most of the currently available editors rely on hard-wired technologies with very little code reuse between editors. Model driven engineering, and specifically generative programming, can be applied in order to ease the development of these editors.

TOPCASED has specified and implemented a simple yet effective MDE based editor generator for the Eclipse EMF/GEF platform. The editors are generated according to the modelling language description (its meta-model), and several models specifying the graphical primitive and interaction are used in order to edit each part of the modelling language.

This approach is multi-staged and based on the Eclipse JET (Java Emitter Template) for code generation. Each stage takes the meta-model as a parameter and a model describing the various aspects of the editor in order to generate Java classes for the handling of the models, a hierarchical editor and then a graphical editor. This approach has been proposed as a contribution to Eclipse GMF ("*Graphical Modelling Framework*") [20].

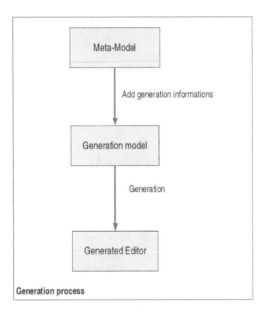

Figure 11.2. *Generation process*

The main requirement for a model editor is to be compliant with the model constraints – defined in the meta-model – and with the usual graphical notation.

A lot of information about the way to edit a model are already in the meta-model and can be used to generate a part of the editor. Other information – like graphical presentation, available diagrams, etc. – is not available in the model. Another model is then used to store the additional parameters needed for the generation. The process to create a new model editor can be split into several steps (Figure 11.2):

- the meta-model definition – using the Ecore modelling language;

- the generation model definition describing the editor behaviour and the graphical information;

- the execution of the generation action provided by TOPCASED. The result of this execution is a functional graphical editor compliant with the input meta-model;

- the last step is optional. It consists of a Java customization of the generated code. During this step the graphical representations can be customized to fit with the requirements of the meta-model specifications.

An example of this process for the Ecore meta-model is given in Figure 11.3.

The graphical editor needs to store graphical information about the current edited model (position of objects, colors, etc.) but these kinds of properties are not defined in the domain meta-model. To solve this problem TOPCASED uses the OMG standard, XMI-DI (XMI – Diagram Interchange).

A simplified view of the XMI-DI model is presented in Figure 11.4.

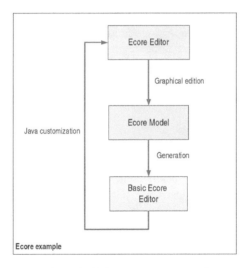

Figure11.3. *Ecore process example*

The XMI-DI model wraps the domain model and adds all the missing information needed to display the model. Using this "graphical" model, we can exchange the diagrams with others modelling tools and export it to external formats (RSM, Together, SVG, etc.).

TOPCASED is based on the Eclipse JET engine (Java Emitter Templates) for code generation. With this generation engine, the generated code can be customized and then re-generated without losing already defined customizations.

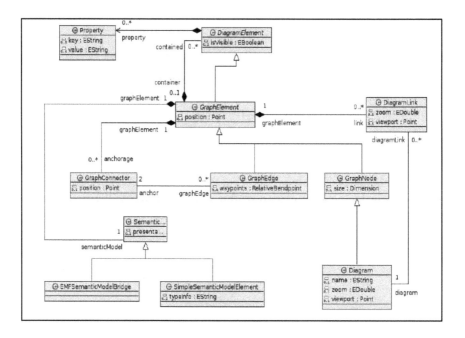

Figure 11.4. *A simplified view of the XMI_DI*

Using TOPCASED and EMF it is also possible to generate Java classes for the handling of the models within Eclipse, a hierarchical editor, documentation reports (HTML, PDF), helper classes to handle context menu, etc. This approach has been proposed as a contribution to Eclipse GMF (Graphical Modelling Framework).

11.5. Acknowledgement

The authors acknowledge the contribution to this work of F. Migeon and X. Thirioux and all the developers and testers from Airbus, Anyware Technologies and CS involved in the project.

11.6. References

[1]   CNRT: *"CNRT-AE: Centre National de Recherche Technologique Aéronautique et Espace"*, URL: http://www.cnrtae.com/ (in French), 2005.

[2]   M. Dahchour, A. Pirotte, E. Zimányi. *"Definition and application of metaclasses"*, in Proceedings of the 12th Int. Conference on Database and Expert Systems Applications, DEXA'01, Munich, Germany, LNCS Vol. 2113, Springer-Verlag, p. 32-41, Sept. 2001.

[3]   Eclipse consortium: *"Eclipse: an extensible development platform and application frameworks for building software"*, URL: http://www.eclipse.org/, 2005.

[4]   EMF project: *"EMF: Eclipse Modelling Framework."*, URL: http://www.eclipse.org/emf/, 2005.

[5]   X. Blanc, M.-P. Gervais, P. Sriplakich, *"Model Bus: Towards the interoperability of modelling tools"*, MDAFA'04, Linköping, 2004.

[6]   Assert project: *"Assert: Automated proof based System and Software Engineering for Real-Time"*, URL: http://www.assert-online.net/, 2005.

[7]   ModelWare project: *"MODELWARE: MODELling solution for softWARE systems"*, European research project (IST), URL: http://www.modelware-ist.org, 2005.

[8]   P.-A. Muller, C. Dumoulin, F. Fondement, M. Hassenforder. *"The TopModL initiative"*, 3rd Workshop in Software Model Engineering, 7th International Conference on the UML (WiSME@UML 2004), Lisbon, Portugal, Oct. 2004.

[9]   B. Berthomieu, P.O Ribet, F. Vernadt, JL Bernartt, J.M Farines,J.P. Bodeveix, M. Filali, G. Padiou, P. Farail, P.Gaufillet, P. Dissaux, J.L. Lambert: *"Towards the verification of real-time systems in avionics: the Cotre approach"*, 8th International Workshop on Formal Methods for Industrial Critical Systems (FMICS'03), Trondheim (Norway), June 2005.

[10]   B. Selic. *"The Pragmatics of Model-Driven Development"*, IEEE Software, Vol. 20(5), Sept. 2003.

[11]   OMG. *"The Common Object Request Broker: Architecture and Specification"*, Revision 2.0, OMG document formal/97-02-25, Jul. 1995 (updated Jul. 1995, until Revision 2.3 June 1999). URL Revision 2.0:

          http://www.omg.org/cgi-bin/apps/doc?formal/97-02-25.pdf. URL Revision 2.3.

          http://www.omg.org/cgi-bin/apps/doc?formal/98-12-01.pdf

[12]   OMG. *"Unified Modeling Language Specification"*, Version 1.5, OMG document formal/03-03-01, Mar. 2003. Available at: http://www.omg.org/cgi-bin/apps/doc?formal/03-03-01.pdf

[13]   A. Kleppe, J. Warmer, W. Bast. *"MDA Explained: The Model Driven Architecture Practice and Promise"*, Addison Wesley, 2003.

[14]   D. Frankel. "*Model Driven Architecture: Applying MDA to Enterprise Computing*", Wiley Press, 2003.

[15]   OMG. "*Meta Object Facility (MOF) Specification*", Version 1.3, OMG document formal/00-04-03, Mar. 2000. URL:

http://www.omg.org/cgi-bin/apps/doc?formal/00-04-03.pdf. URL Version 1.4:

http://www.omg.org/cgi-bin/apps/doc?formal/02-04-03.pdf

[16]   ISO, Information Technology. "*Information Resource Dictionary System (IRDS) Framework*", standard ISO/IEC 10027, 1990 (and ISO/IEC 10728, 1993).

[17]   EIA. "*Framework for Modeling and Extensibility*", Extract of Interim Standard, EIA/IS-107, Electronics Industries Association, CDIF Technical Committee, Jan. 1994.

[18]   Tni Europe: "*Sildex: a formal approach to real-time applications development*", URL: http://www.tni-world.com/rtbuilder.asp, 2005.

[19]   A. Canals, C. Le Camus, M. Feau, G. Jolly, V. Bonafous, P. Bazavan: "*An operational use of ATL: integration of the model transformation in the TOPCASED project*", ICSSEA'2005 Conf., 2005.

[20]   GMF project: "*GMF: the Graphical Modelling Framework*", URL: http://www.eclipse.org/gmf/, 2005.

11.7. Glossary

AADL   *Architecture Analysis and Design Language*

EMF   *Eclipse Modelling Framework*

EMFT   *EMF Tools*

GEF   *Graphical Editor Framework (part of Eclipse)*

GMF   *Graphical Modeller Framework (part of Eclipse)*

GMT   *Generative Modelling Framework (part of Eclipse)*

HOOD   *Hierarchical Object Oriented Design*

MDA   *Model Driven Architecture (part of OMG)*

MDE   *Model Driven Engineering*

MOF   *Meta-Object Facility (part of OMG)*

OCL   *Object Constraint Language (part of OMG)*

OMG   *Object Management Group*

TOPCASED   *Toolkit in Open source for Critical Aeronautic SystEms Design*

UML   *Unified Modelling Language (part of OMG)*

XMI   *XML Metadata Interchange (part of OMG)*

XML   *Extensible Markup Language*

CHAPTER 12

Facing Industrial Challenges: A Return on an Experiment on Model-driven Engineering

Chapter written by Jean-Luc Voirin

THALES Aerospace
Brest, France
www.thalesgroup.com
jean-luc.voirin@fr.thalesgroup.com

12.1. Introduction

This chapter describes an industrial experiment of model-driven engineering (MDE) concepts, deployed in complex developments, and their returns on experiments, seen from an industrial company.

After a brief presentation of the context and motivations to explore MDE, and a quick overview on what MDE means in our context, we list some initially expected benefits from the approach; then we give some examples of industrial use of MDE in aerospace systems, and findings based on these experiments.

The Need for Architectures and Model Driven Engineering

Anybody can see today that electronic equipment has become not only more and more powerful, but also complex, either to be used or to deliver expected service; this is not only true in home appliance and consumer electronics, but of course even more so in complex systems, such as aircraft and related embedded systems or equipment, which must comply with stringent constraints such as safety, security, ergonomics, reliability, cost, etc.

This growing complexity deeply impacts on systems engineering and design, in many fields: functional need and requirements, product design constraints above, technologies to be assessed, ever increasing size of development teams, and time to market are all more and more sources of added engineering complexity – and furthermore intricated, which requires new practices to master, ease, secure, structure product engineering, etc.

Current trends in engineering practices address this through two complementary ways: Architecture-centric and Model-driven Engineering.

Architecture-driven Engineering

The first approach, and the most immediately promising, is to organize and manage the product Engineering through a structuring Architecture ("Architecture-driven Engineering"):

Identify main Architectural Drivers (major architectural Properties expected from the product, such as fault tolerance, dynamic modularity, etc.), along with Architectural Patterns (templates, such as plug-in components, services, data flow pipes, etc.), to structure product Architecture, to strengthen and guide Engineering, to favour and secure Reuse. Architecture helps in confining complexity, in separating concerns, in standardizing development practices and design solutions.

Yet Architecture still remains complex to build, understand, use and apply in the product development: it appears necessary, but often not enough to hide, manage, master complexity.

Method and rules are also necessary to design according to the architecture concepts, along with templates to support the method and to speed up the design, and tools to assist and automate the teaming development process.

Model-driven Engineering

For this purpose, a second approach, considered as complementary to Architecture-centric Engineering, intends to use simplified, more easily manageable views of the system, each one eventually dealing with specific design issues: in a few words, build and exploit appropriate models of the architecture and product ("Model-driven Engineering"). This document focuses on this approach, which could be summarized this way: "Build an Architecture-centric, Model-driven, Tooled-up Engineering Process".

12.2. A quick overview of our understanding of MDE

Although taking great benefit from academic work around MDE, we do not intend to apply it "as is", but instead, we start from our industrial need and try to capture in the MDE "philosophy" elements to sustain our own approach. This is why part of our own view of MDE as applied in our organization may seem distorted when compared to academic tenets and concepts around MDE.

As considered in our business – and in order to be applicable to its wide area of products and domains – a model is seen as a simplified, formalized representation of a system (or software), able to illustrate system composition, behaviour, properties, etc. more easily than looking at the system itself.

Main selected features of Model-driven Engineering in this context can be summarized, to some extent, as follows:

– The use of models to define and manage development (instead of documentation, blueprints or code);

– Formal representations of these models, based on non-ambiguous and consistent, checkable languages;

– Adoption of models, but strictly and only if based on a structuring Architecture, in a domain-dependent context (Use-Cases, Need, functional and non-functional constraints);

– Methods and rules to build and check models, according to the domain-dependent context;

– Tools to automate model checking, model transformation, code generation from a design model.

The following table, a kind of "MDE Quiz", gives some criteria to evaluate MDE compliance of engineering practices (in the Thales Aerospace context, as defined above).

Questions	Related MDE concepts	Check!
can your product needs and architecture be described using only a reduced set of "patterns"? (e.g. components, functions, services)	Meta-model (patterns)	☐
are these patterns well defined, formalised, shareable?	Formalised Description Language and Concepts	☐
are there well defined rules for the use of these patterns? For the global system definition?	Meta-Model Grammar and Rules, Profiles, etc.	☐
are these rules sufficient to guide and secure the system engineering?	Model Checking	☐
are there rules to check consistency of the system description wrt the model patterns?	Checking via Meta-Model	☐
are there separate models for system design and execution platform? Or at least, is the system design model independent from platform issues?	Platform Independent/ Specific Models (PIM, PSM)	☐
are there rules for mapping the system design model onto the platform? More generally, to help or automate transition and links form one model to another? (e.g. code generation, simulation, etc.)	Model Transformation	☐

Table 12.1. *MDE Quiz*

12.3. Expected Benefits of Model-driven Engineering

Introducing new methods, developing adapted support tools, and more important, deploying and supporting them "in the large" towards the whole community of engineers, is costly for any company, and therefore must be considered from a "Return on Investment" (ROI) point of view.

Some benefits requested from MDE, in order to obtain this return on investment in an industrial context, are as follows.

Ease and guide Development

Formalized architectural patterns (incl. meta-models) help to guide and ease design and development: the use of models of the product architecture, including pre-defined patterns, profiles, etc., is intended to help in applying design method and correct use of architecture.

Early maturity by assessing and fixing engineering and integration issues should also be possible at model level, thanks to the exploitation of models for early validation (at least through models simulation and execution means).

Secure Engineering

Models are intended to give a means to materialise and formalize (and even impose) architecture concepts, and associated method and rules, giving concrete means to manipulate, experiment and check all of them, as mentioned above.

However, they can also be used as means to control the design to check common good practices and recommendations, through model checking against design rules.

The ability to automate description and generation of interfaces, behaviour, and more generally "integration contracts" for architectural components may also reduce risk to introduce "hand-made" errors.

Improve Productivity

A strong contribution to competitiveness can be expected from automation in production of various engineering assets from a formalized detailed design model (by model transformation): automatic code generation, assistance/automation of tests and validation phases (at least through traceability links between models), etc.

Model-driven Engineering should be a cornerstone in capitalization and reuse: domain knowledge, use cases, architecture patterns, product line constraints, etc., may also be formalised in reusable models.

Ease multi-company Development and Reuse

Concurrent engineering can be clearly allocated and managed through models, favouring formally supported common process, same modelling languages, and easily exchangeable models; in this context, control and check capabilities described above are also of prime importance.

Be independent from Technology Changes

Formalized models are expected to be independent from execution platform, language, COTS; as an example, change of target platform/technology should have little impact and cost, through code generators modification.

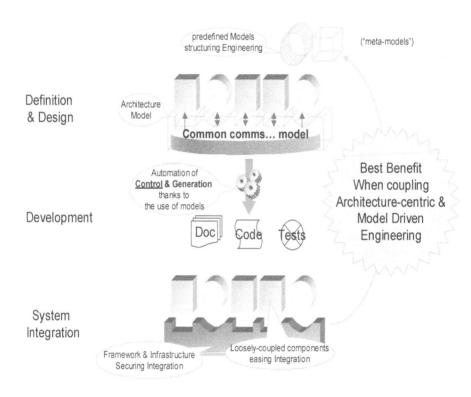

Figure 12.1. *A quick sketch of MDE Benefits*

12.4. Applying MDE Concepts in an industrial Context

The use of Model-driven Engineering concepts in an industrial context, as defined above, will be illustrated through three application domains.

Signal processing (SP) for complex sensors (radars, electronic intelligence, self-protection, etc.) necessitates a huge processing power, usually addressed through massively parallel computing. Issues such as algorithm tuning, and algorithm mapping on target multi-processor, are particularly complex engineering activities.

Graphics processing for navigation instruments cockpit display (CD) in the cockpit of a commercial aircraft is safety-critical, potentially subject to complex ergonomics tuning during the whole lifecycle of the product, and yet must respect stringent constraints in terms of standards, behavior rules, etc.

Tactical Command and Control Systems (C2), in a combat or surveillance aircraft, are in charge of managing the mission, delivering human-system interfaces (HIS) to the crew, interfacing sensors, building a tactical view of the scene and delivering weapons when necessary. They have to process thousands of pieces of information, in real-time, adapting to various and variable missions, system modes, etc.

Note that these applications of MDE concepts have been deployed in a real program, full scale, industrial process, and not only on toy problems.

Reference Architecture and Patterns

In a signal processing (SP) context, architecture is mainly data flow-driven: elementary processing and reusable items are triggered by the data flow; they are composed as required by algorithms, then parallelised on a multi-processor execution platform, in order to ensure requested performance. The reference architecture formalizes processing items, communication and synchronisation means between them, along with contents and formats of data flows.

Cockpit display (CD) is seen as a graphics server, managing graphical elementary objects (altitude or speed scale, horizon, etc.), e.g. applying a MVC (Model View Controller) pattern. Graphical objects have a predefined behavior, features and "look and feel", and must react either to system changes (e.g. altitude increase) or to crew interaction (e.g. altitude alert threshold selection).

Command and Control Systems (C2) are built from processing components, including sensors and weapons interfaces, HSI parts, data processing, and shared tactical view, in a layered, loosely coupled architecture. Components may be activated or even plugged-in depending on the mission phase, required cooperation between them, etc. They mainly interact through shared information models, services, and notification means. When hard real-time constraints occur, a separate description of the real-time architecture and scheduling is built, not interfering with the functional components description, thanks to adequate architectural properties.

Domain dependent Models

SP models are based on data flow diagrams (DFD) combining reusable elementary processing items, along with typed data flows carrying synchronisation conditions. A separate model contains description of the execution platform composition and topology.

CD Models are partly graphical description (built with a graphics "wysiwyg" editor) for the view part, and partly behavioral (automata, formal synchronous languages), for the functional specification. Both are linked through object attributes and formalized definition of external interfaces in a complementary model, and objects are accessible in a reuse library.

C2 models are fully described in UML, using dedicated profiles: component model including a generic framework, shared information model, available services, and their mutual interactions in the overarching architecture of the C2.

Engineering Rules on Models

For each of the models above, an associated "know-how" is formalized as design rules, in order to guide their building: for example, boundaries of elementary processing items in order to ease their efficient mapping on target; nature and orientation of dependencies between components or services in order to ease integration and loose coupling; information model building rules in order to maximise shared data access performance; requirements on components behaviour to enable hot swap in case of failure, etc.

Model checking

Models are checked against former design rules as much as possible, in order to early detect defects or misuse of the reference architecture.

However, they can also help in early checking of some expected properties of the final product: as an example, when some provision of each elementary processing performance is available and introduced in the models, tools exploiting and "weaving" the various models (e.g. description, behavior, real-time architecture) can check that a given real-time architecture (activation and scheduling patterns) is compliant with expected input-to-output latencies and global performance.

Platform Independence

All three domains use layered architectures separating design and implementation concerns: target languages (C, C++, Java, Ada95 depending on domains) can be selected as needed after modeling; mapping on target execution platform is independent and after modeling; model is (partly) validated before target implementation, and execution can be driven either on target or on general purpose host computers.

Model Transformation

Model transformation is broadly used for platform mapping and code generation (but has to deal with certification constraints on generation tools): generating communication code and processing elements allocation to processors in SP (including configuration and deployment files definition), generating graphics and behavioral code for CD, and the whole for C2. In the latter case, a formal model transformation is used to generate code adapted to different technologies and targets.

Another use of model transformation is to build simulation models related to the design, either by making design models executable, or by defining transformations targeting dedicated simulation environments, formal languages, etc.

In some cases, model transformation also helps to generate test environments and patterns for components, collect metrics on software, predict performance.

Figure 12.2 gives a simple example of using MDE concepts.

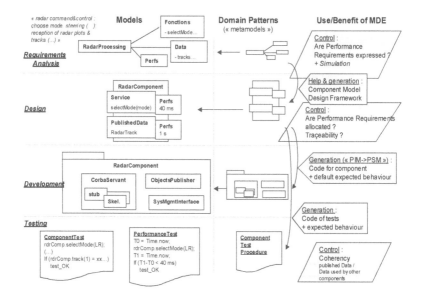

Figure 12.2. *Example of MDE Concepts Use*

12.5. Return of Experiment and Findings on MDE Use

MDE Findings: general considerations

General, multi-domain findings based on the former experiments and deployment might be summarized as follows:

"MDE does not make you more clever, but more efficient".

MDE does not guide engineering by itself, but instead proposes a general purpose "framework", to be customized to fit domain-dedicated process requirements, in which the domain-dependent know-how has to be formalized.

It is of no use without:

- a well-defined architecture;

- a clear engineering method and design rules;

- a proven engineering process sustaining both;

- that should pre-exist prior to MDE deployment.

Under these conditions, MDE may be of great help in:

– asking the good engineering questions,

– giving a frame to formalize answers,

– and building one's own response while easing and empowering its tooling.

MDE favours building an architectural approach and searching for "Invariants", therefore easing reuse and capitalization.

Furthermore, MDE is not necessarily UML: in the examples above, UML is only used in one case; other formalisms can be used in a model-driven approach, as shown.

MDE Findings: perceived benefits

As mentioned, MDE is seen as a good support to our architecture-centric engineering strategy, through the use of [meta]models, patterns, transformation rules, supporting the expression and building of architectural assets. It appears as a necessary framework to guide design and architecture use/reuse.

MDE contributes to the management of engineering complexity, since it is a good way to hide this design complexity in some cases (simplify the use of architecture, middleware issues, projection on platform and technologies, etc.).

MDE can also contribute to maintain better consistency between requirements and design, through automatic links and transformations between models, impact analysis thanks to these links.

More generally, MDE can constitute a bridge and a means to unify modeling, simulation, production, testing and (early) validation issues, provided that each of them can exploit common models through different views and exploitation means.

The benefit of automatic code generation, test tools generation, etc. has also been mentioned earlier, and can probably be much extended in coming years.

MDE Findings: perceived issues

In spite of the former benefits, some difficulties arose concerning MDE use in an industrial context.

Manipulating Models

Models are easier than code to help designers and other stakeholders understand and build a System or software, but today model implementations cannot be fully substituted to code.

For design/coding, at a certain level of detail, code is often more expressive, and easier to manipulate (reuse, cut and paste, etc.); furthermore, models are hardly subject to optimisation (resource consumption, performance, etc.), as code is.

Models (automatic) testing, validation, configuration management, are harder to implement and therefore more difficult today. As a consequence, for software engineering, two references are still to link, to maintain and to synchronize models and code.

Furthermore, when entering tests and integration phases, only code is accessible e.g. in debuggers, which introduce a brutal break of abstraction level; hiding complexity and technological issues becomes impossible, which results in significant trouble in debug and integration phases.

Cost of a full automated model-driven process

Gaining benefit from automatic generation and model transformation may be a long, huge and complex work that should not be underestimated:

– even if a well-defined Architecture, a clear Engineering Method and Design Rules, and a proven Engineering Process sustaining both (as mentioned earlier) already exist, defining the appropriate meta-models is complex and should be entrusted to experts; transformation rules are to be created accordingly, in the same way and should impact meta-model definition, therefore making the process more complex;

– and implementation of the whole of this through generators, meta-modellers, etc., is up to now far from being straightforward and easy, given the fact that these tools are critical for the whole products generation (see development and debugging of compilers as an analogy).

Furthermore, any weakness in one of these will result in a heavy price to be paid, due to the difficulty to locate problems (meta-models, modelling, transformation rules, transformation engines, code generators, etc.).

The middle of the road

Of course, the benefits of model-driven approach do not rely only on code generation, for example, so that some might think of stopping the adoption process when return on invest becomes uncertain. One problem is that stopping in the middle of the road may be costly and increase complexity for developers, instead of reducing it: some design and architecture choices are only acceptable because the complexity of their bringing into play is hidden, and partly assumed by transformation/generation tools.

Tools are still expected...

From the former comments, it can be concluded that efficiency largely relates on toolset capability, for MDE approaches (in the same way as good development environments can greatly ease the use of some language); unfortunately, existing toolsets are still weak in this context:

– few truly address meta-modelling, transformation means and rules support; their capabilities have still not reached those of conventional system and software engineering tools,

– and furthermore they are not integrated in an overarching tools architecture supporting industrial processes (e.g. documentation generation and management, models configuration management, link with requirements, certified tools and generators, etc.): the tools market appears not to be mature.

Extending MDE to a wider scope

MDE is initially focused on Software dominant and/or Information systems; therefore it cannot easily be applied "as is" to different activities and domains in the same way and to the same extent; at least, much work is to be done to address systems engineering issues beyond functional modelling (this point is beyond the scope of this paper; see e.g. ARTEMIS research agenda for real-time embedded systems engineering issues).

Modeling: the Holy Grail?

Modeling should not be considered as the ultimate goal and means to build the expected product. Current trends in model-driven engineering, possibly in academic research, focus more on how to represent (model) either need or solution, than how to build these representations, and make the solution emerge. The whole process of engineering – solution building – should be considered as a whole, focusing also on supporting the intellectual process and reasoning towards the solution, including rules and methods to build and validate each stage of the process.

Cost of adoption

Last but not least, MDE requires a significant effort on training, dissemination, support, to be fully exploited and correctly used (modeling language, tools use, process, etc.).

12.6. Conclusion: so what about MDE?

MDE is no silver bullet, and should be considered as a means rather than an end; using it alone on a non-structured engineering approach may be worse than doing nothing.

Yet the industry still has to face an increasing complexity of systems and of their requirements, ever-growing development teams and foreign partnerships, support for product policy and reuse issues, etc. There are strong needs for a secured engineering, and for that purpose, MDE may be of great help, even outside software dominant systems.

It can be used as a means to help structuring engineering, and an incentive to:

– formalize and concentrate on functional and architectural points of view first;

– separate concerns (functional, non-functional and technical);

– use models when appropriate, especially for:

- supporting architectural and product line approach;

- guiding and constraining each phase (pre-defined patterns, structure and guidelines instead of starting from scratch);

- checking the products of each phase against rules and expected practices;

- assisting or automating transition from one phase to another (thanks to formalised models and transformation rules upon them).

INDEX OF AUTHORS

Printed in the USA
CPSIA information can be obtained
at www.ICGtesting.com
CBHW050722241124
17264CB00001B/1